Holistic Philosophy 101

By
Mishaal Talib Mahfuz El Bey
All Rights Reserved

Moorish Americans - Northwest Amexem

Black & White Edition

Holistic Philosophy 101
Black & White Edition

© 2020
CALIFA MEDIA PUBLISHING
LAFAYETTE, IN

ISBN-13: 978-1-952828-83-6

BY
MISHAAL TALIB MAHFUZ EL BEY

All Rights Reserved, Without Prejudice. No Part of This Book May Be Reproduced Or Transmitted In Any Form, By Any Means Electronic, Photocopying, Mechanical, Recording, Information Storage, Or Retrieval System Unless for The Liberation Of Minds And Gaining Of Knowledge Of Self.

Califa Media™
A Moorish Guide Publishing Company
califamedia.com
All Rights, Remedies & Liberties Reserved

Holistic Philosophy 101

Works Cited:

- Traditional Chinese Medicine: An authoritative and comprehensive guide Henry C. Lu, PH. D
- Ancient herbs and modern medicine- Henry Han, O.M.D., Glenn E. Miller, M.D., Nancy Deville
- Dr.alimelbey.com
- How to study-Taj Tarik Bey via RvBeypublications.com
- Sacred Sexuality Ancient Egyptian Tantric Yoga- Dr. Muata Ashby
- Ancient Secret of the flower of life- Drunvalo Melchizedek
- The Art of War- Sun Tzu
- King Alfred Plan Rex84- RvBeypublications.com
- Outwitting the Devil- Napoleon Hill
- Russell Rules: 11 lessons on leadership- Bill Russell with David Falkner
- Metu Neter volume 1 & 2- Ra Un Nefer Amen
- 12 Powers of Man- Charles Fillmore
- Skyycrystals.com
- The Art of Peace- Morihei Ueshiba
- The Perfection of Yoga- A.C. Bhaktivedanta
- The Cave of the Ancients- Tuesday Lobsang Rampa
- The Heart's Code- Paul Pearsall, Ph.D.
- Breath, Mind and consciousness-Harish Johari
- Science of Breath: A Practical Guide- Swami Rama, Rudolph Ballentine, M.D. and Allan Hymes, M.D.
- A COMPLETE GUIDE TO CHI-GUNG: Harnessing the Power of the Universe- Daniel Reid

2Holistic Philosophy 101
Contents

Introduction:	1
Part 1: (W)Holiness of Th Temple	2
Chapter 1: Wealth	2
(A) Principles of naturopathy	2
(B) Reflexology	3
Chapter 2: 5 Distinct characteristics of traditional Chinese Medicine	5
Chapter 3: Energy	6
(A). Qi [Chi]: Knowing the flow	6
(B) The Three Treasures:	6
(C) Basic Principles of Qi:	6
(D) 3 sources of Q:	6
(E) Basic movement of Qi:	9
(F) Basic Functions of Qi:	9
(G) Classifications of Qi:	10
(H) Basic Modes of Moving Energy:	11
(I) Chi-gung: Pillar of Life	13
(J) Vital Substances	14
Chapter 4: Yin and Yang: Restoring Balance	15
Chapter 5: Causes of Disease	22
Chapter 6: Exercise	25
Chapter 7: Meditation: 100 benefits	30
Part 2: Moral Intelligence	47
Chapter 1: Science	48
(A) Knowing Self-7 aspects of study	48
(B) How to study	49
(C) Think Before You speak: Process of Elimination	50
Chapter 2: Reconnecting the hemispheres	51
(A) Dimensional Awareness	51
(B) Wisdom of the East	56
Chapter 3: The Art of War	61
(A) Laying Plans	61
(B) Attack by stratagem	62
(C) Variation in tactics	63
Chapter 4: King Alfred Plan	63
(A) Silent weapons for quiet wars	63
(B) Historical Introduction	64
(C) Political Introduction	65
(D) Energy	66
(E) Theoretical introduction	68
(F) General energy concepts	68
(G) Rothschild's energy discovery	69
(H) Apparent capital as "paper" inductor	70
(I) Breakthrough	70
(J) Application in economics	71
(K) Summary	71
(L) Short List of inputs	73
Chapter 5: Outwitting the Devil	79
(A) Self-Defense	79
(B) Education	80
(C) Disharmony/Self-sabotage	82
(E) 6 fears of man	83
(F) Controlled Sex	84
(G) Fear and Faith	84
(H) 9 gates of hell	85
(I) 7 principles of freedom (Heaven)	85
(J) Self-Diagnosis	86
Chapter 6: 11 Lessons on Leadership	88
(A) Curiosity	88
(B) Ego	88
(C) Listening	89
(D) Toughness or tenderness: creating your leadership style	90
(E) Invisibility	90

- (F) Craftsmanship — 91
- (G) Personal integrity — 91
- (H) Rebounding — 92
- (I) Imagination — 92
- (J) Discipline, delegation, and decision-making — 92
- (K) Everyone can win — 93

Chapter 7: THE 24 DOMINANT LAWS OF THE SUBCONSCIOUS MIND by Lloyd Dison — 93

Part 3: G.O.D.-Generator, Operator, Destroyer — 99

Chapter 1: Stages of Spiritual Growth — 100

Chapter 2: The manifestation of God in Man — 101

Chapter 3: Spiritual Eyes — 102

Chapter 4: The Force of 12 — 106
- (A) 12 powers of man (galactic) — 106
- (B) The 12 apostles (heavenly) — 112
- (C) 12 Ideals of perfected man (earthly) — 114

Chapter 5: The 7's — 116
- (A) The 7 chakras — 116
- (B) The 7 spiritual laws — 146
- (C) The 7 steps of manifestation — 148

Chapter 6: The Art of Peace — 148

Chapter 7: Yoga (union) — 154
- (A) Chemistry — 154
- (B) The Resurrection — 158
- (C) Completing the cir*cle*/*circuit*: — 173
- (D) Heart, soul, and science: — 174

Outro — 176

Final word — 178

The Golden Rule — 179

Introduction:

What is wealth? The Answer is health, naturally as such is the prerequisite to a productive and fulfilling life. So, then what does it mean to be healthy? Is it simply a nutritious pattern of eating? Is it meditation? Is it positive thinking. Mantras and affirmations? Is it a sense of humor? Is it communion/good associations? Is it objectivity? It is all the above. All these methods combine to form what is deemed balance, and such is perfection. "Ascension" is achieved by the four c's: control (self), courage, compassion and creativity. These when tempered with sincerity and consistency lead to progression/evolution. This collection of philosophies was compiled for the stimulation and ultimately the activation of the divine self, leading to the restoration and elevation of our lost (e)state of divine love consciousness. Now I am not a guru, nor am I a licensed clinician or attempting to be anything other than a concerned citizen of this Earth who has found some info that I think is worthy of public attention. Like you, brothers and sisters, I am striving for divine understanding, wisdom and knowledge and occasionally I have and do stumble on this path but in all sincerity, I believe in the power and effectiveness of right knowledge, so I offer this as a means to provide a guide for those seeking to simplify yet at the same time elevate their lives. Much respect and appreciation to you, yours and ours as a collective. Peace be upon the peaceable, love to the lovers and strength to the warriors.

Part 1: (W)Holiness of Th Temple

*The blissing, o man, of thy external part is health, vigor and proportion. The greatest of these is health. What health is to the body even that is honesty to the soul. -Holy Koran Circle 7, CHAPTER 38 HOLY INSTRUCTIONS FROM THE PROPHET THE SOUL OF MAN

Chapter 1: Wealth

(A) Principles of naturopathy

1. The healing power of nature (vis medicatrix naturae). Naturopathic physicians believe and know that the body has considerable power to heal itself. It is the role of the physician to facilitate and enhance this process with the aid of natural non-toxic therapies.

2. Identify and treat the cause (tolle causam). The naturopathic physician is trained to seek the underlying causes of a disease rather than simply suppress the symptoms, which are viewed as expressions of the body's attempt to heal. The causes of disease can arise at the physical, mental-emotional, and spiritual levels.

3. First, do no harm (primum non nocere). The naturopathic physician seeks to do no harm with medical treatment by employing safe and effective natural therapies.

4. Treat the whole being (holism). Naturopathic physicians are trained to view an individual as a whole, a complex interaction of physical, mental-emotional, spiritual, social, and other factors.

5. The physician as teacher (docere). The naturopathic physician is foremost a teacher, educating, empowering, and motivating the patients to assume more personal responsibility for their health by adopting a healthful attitude, lifestyle, and eating habits.

6. Prevention is the best cure. Naturopathic physicians are specialists in preventative medicine. Prevention of disease and support of health are accomplished through education and life habits.

7. Establishing health and wellness. Establishing and maintaining optimal health and promoting wellness are the most important objectives of the naturopathic physician. While health is defined as the state of optimal physical, mental, emotional, and spiritual wellbeing, wellness is defined as a state of health characterized by a positive emotional state. The naturopathic

8. physician strives to increase the level of wellness regardless of the disease or level of health. Even in cases of severe disease, a high level of wellness can often be achieved.

(B) Reflexology

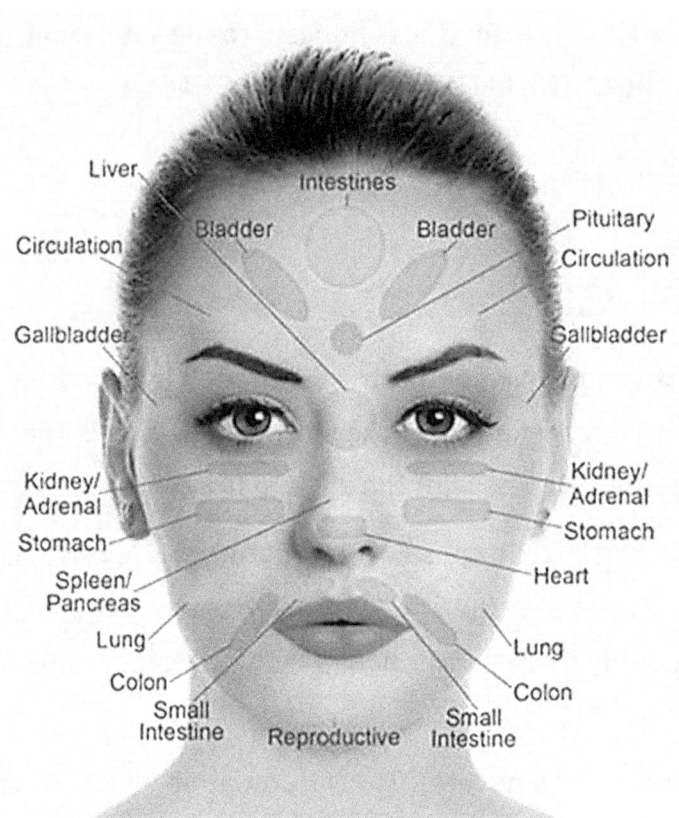

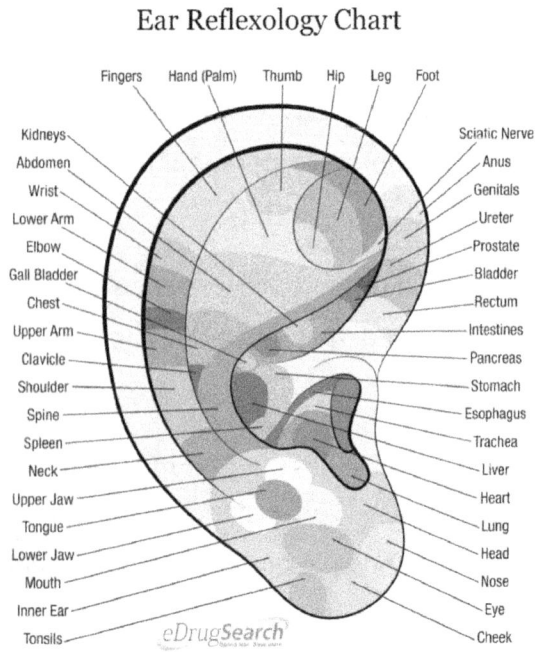

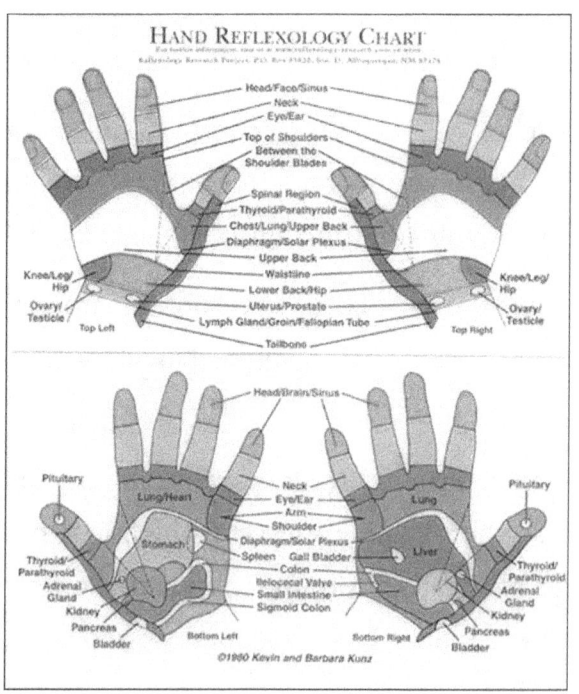

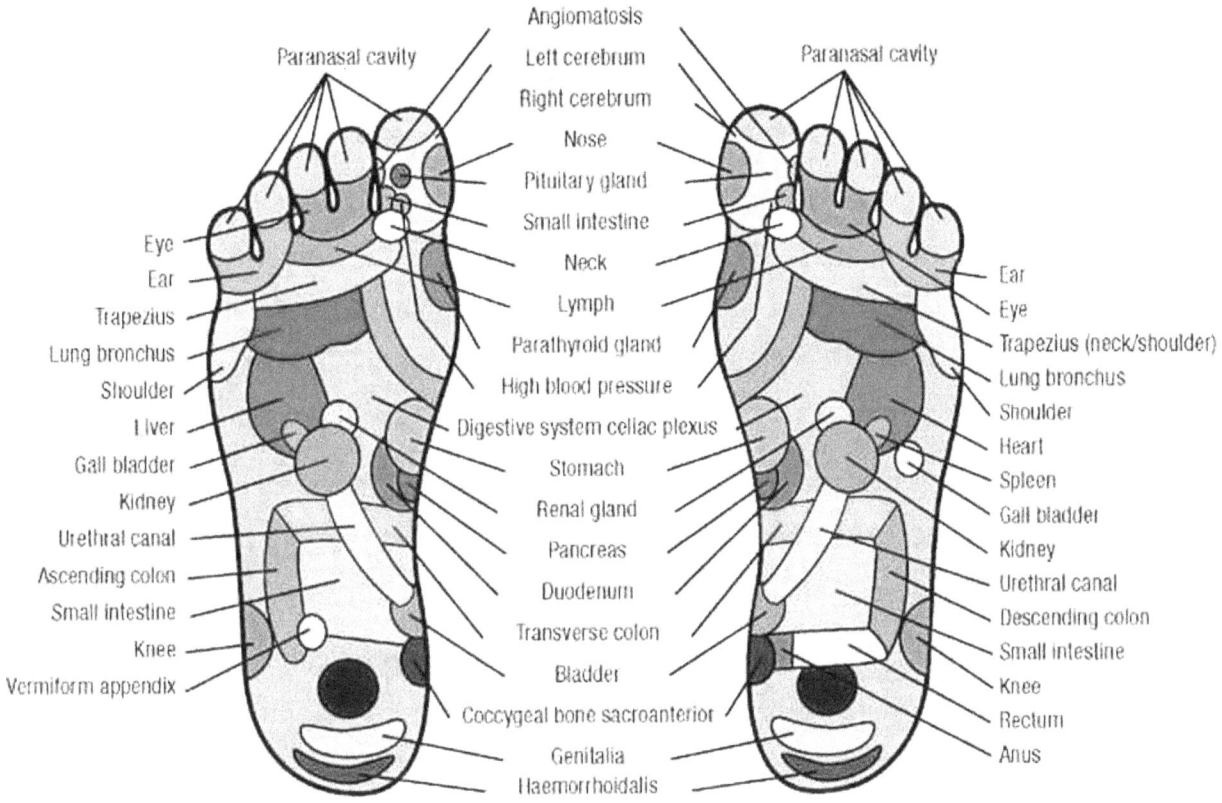

Chapter 2: 5 Distinct characteristics of traditional Chinese Medicine

"A sage will prevent disease rather than cure it, maintain order rather than correct disorder, which is the ultimate principle of wisdom. To cure a disease with medicines is like digging a well when one is already thirsty, it is like making weapons when the war has already broken out, which could be too late to do much good."

1. Simplicity: Saves time and makes self-healing not only possible but also enjoyable. For example, by following a simple recipe of food cures that you can prepare at home, you will enjoy a good meal. You can also learn how to give yourself a message when you are worn out or sick. You can also practice various forms of exercise to cure illness and promote good health.

2. Diversity: TCM offers a wide variety of therapies to choose from, depending on your convenience and preference. You may prefer to be treated by acupuncture rather than herbs, for example.

3. Individuality: TCM attaches great importance to individuality in physical makeup. Individuals are distinct from one another, both physically and psychologically, and this difference is addressed in TCM. We all have different ways of thinking, different habits, and different emotions, but in the field of health we tend to forget about the importance of individuality.

4. Wholeness: TCM focuses on the whole body instead of its parts. When making a diagnosis, a doctor of traditional Chinese medicine is concerned with the whole being. The doctor does not treat your stomach at the expense of your liver or vice versa, nor does the doctor treat your arthritis with drugs that cause damage to your heart. The physician focuses on physical and psychological wholeness as key indicators of health and disease. Included in the procedure are questioning the patient, making tongue and pulse diagnosis, coupled with itemizing current symptoms and recording a detailed history. This procedure allows the doctor to piece together the patterns of imbalance, which are used to formulate a diagnosis and recommend treatment specific to the individual patient. Traditional Chinese medicine is not aimed at relieving symptoms on a piecemeal basis, but rather, it directs its attention to treating the underlying cause of the disease and thus returns the body to its balanced and harmonious state.

5. Effectiveness: The effectiveness of TCM is impressive. Recent studies in North America, Australia, and Europe demonstrate the effectiveness and increasingly widespread use of TCM around the world. Most of the clinical studies have concentrated on acupuncture.

Chapter 3: Energy

(A). Qi [Chi]: Knowing the flow

In a cosmic sense, Qi is viewed as the basic substance (mass or matter), as well as the energy necessary to create the physical world, which includes all living things/beings. As explained by western medicine, throughout the universe mass can be connected to energy, and energy can be converted to mass- for example, the food we eat is converted to energy, and burning wood creates the energy of fire/heat. From an oriental perspective, Qi is the singular common bond that exists and connects all living things, thereby being able to pass back and forth and interact. In fact, Qi is not only the common bond between all living things but also the commonality shared by all existence. Qi cannot be destroyed, it can only be transformed from one form to another.

(B) The Three Treasures:

- Jing: prenatal essence; vitality; procreative energy.
- Qi: universal life force that surrounds, permeates, and binds everything.
- Shen: spirit that has the potential to become immortal.

(C) Basic Principles of Qi:

- Qi is dynamic in nature, in that it is constantly moving (circulating) and changing (transforming).
- Qi is always striving to attain balance and harmony.
- Qi involves the constant movement of yin and yang, two mutually dependent opposites.

(D) 3 sources of Q:

- Qi is genetically inherited. Your genetically inherited Qi is made up primarily of kidney energy and determines your constitutional uniqueness and strength.

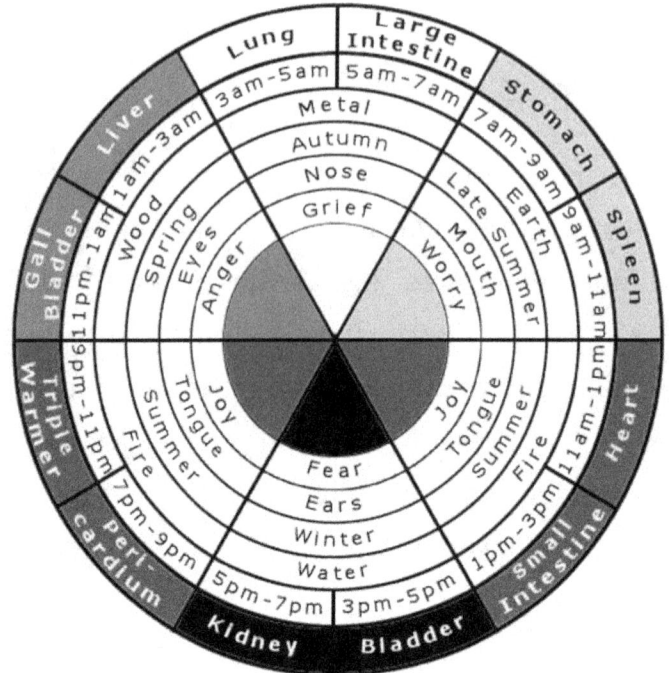

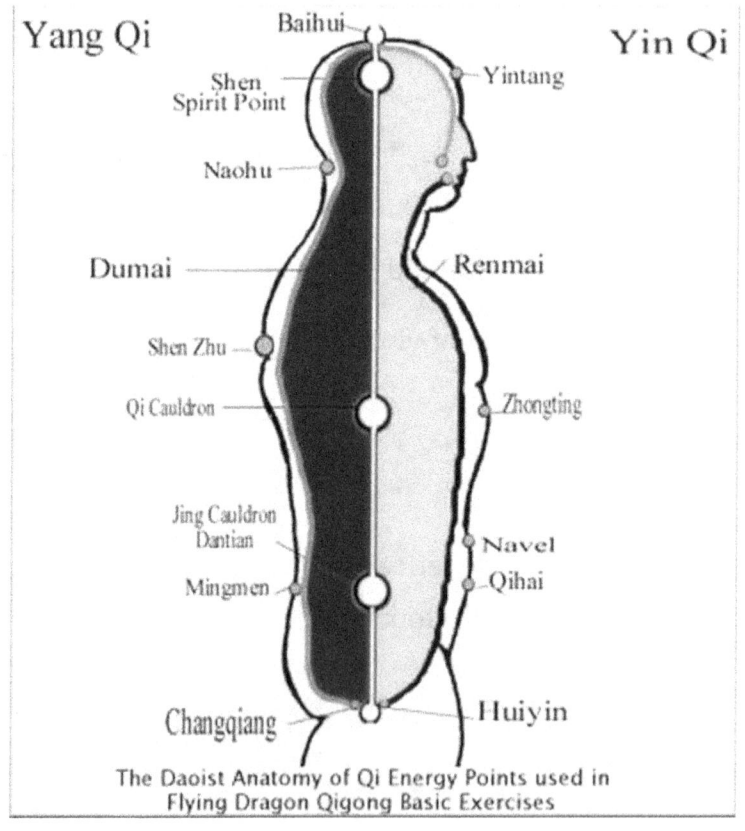

The Daoist Anatomy of Qi Energy Points used in Flying Dragon Qigong Basic Exercises

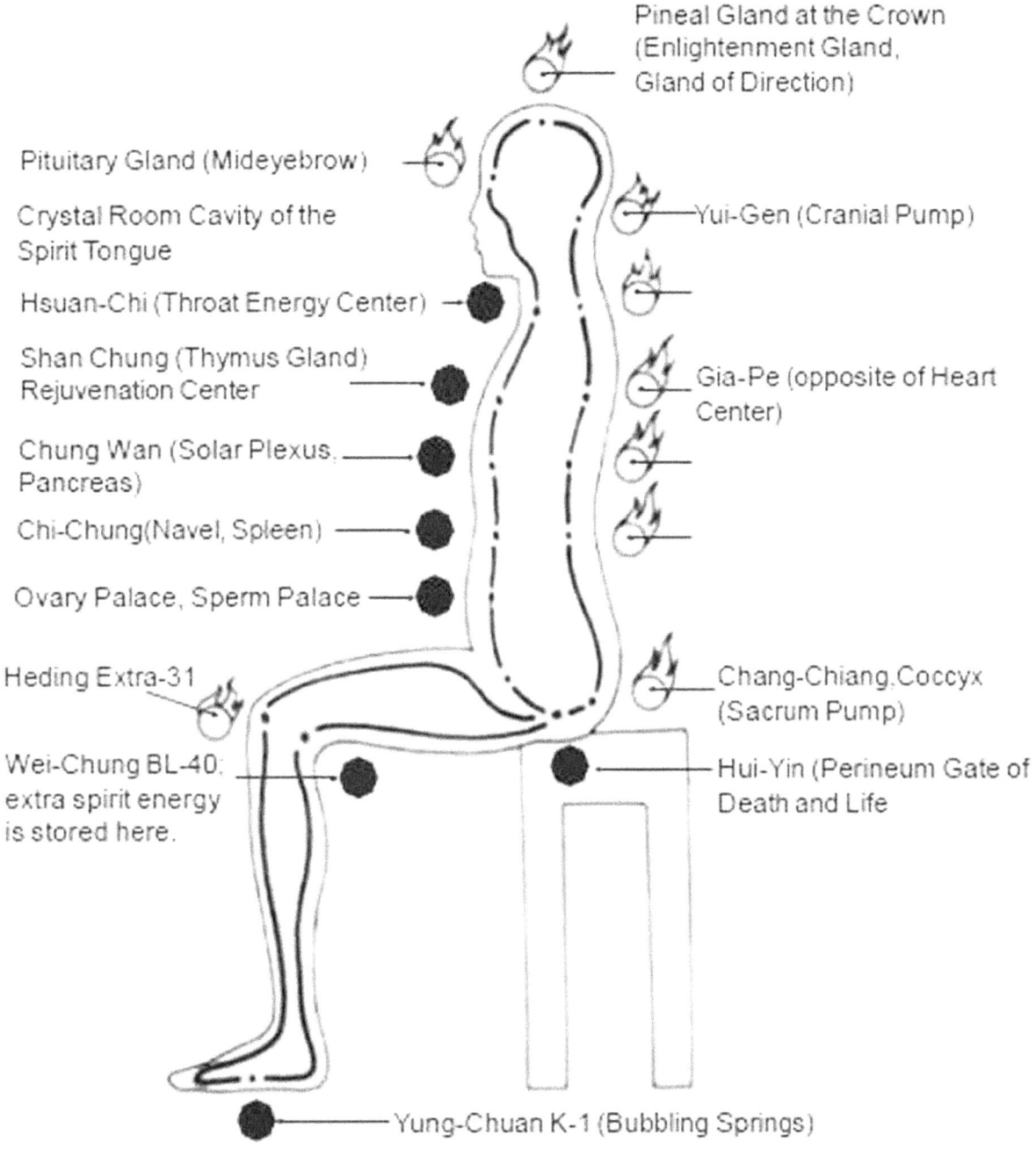

- Qi is acquired internally through your body's functional activities, such as converting nutrients from food sources via digestion. This source of Qi is made up primarily of spleen energy.
- Qi is acquired from the air (oxygen) via lung energy.

Once integrated within your body through the actions of these 3 sources, Qi is then distributed throughout the body and to all other energetic systems to sustain their functions and activities.

(E) Basic movement of Qi

- Ascending- Qi distributes and spreads nutrients and oxygen throughout your body as it ascends.
- Descending- Qi passes down metabolic waste and toxins for elimination and can also deliver nutrients as it descends.
- Inward/Outward- Qi supports and strengthens your body through inward movement. Qi dispenses nutrients and expels toxins through outward movement.
- Circulating- Qi circulates. In other words, energy or the life force circulates within our body.

(F) Basic Functions of Qi:

- Powers the circulation of energy. Qi is the source of the dynamics within your body.
- Regulates the energy movement. Qi acts as the traffic controller, directing the various energy systems throughout the body.
- Nourishes your body. Qi delivers nutrients throughout your body.
- Detoxifies your body. Qi removes toxins and metabolic waste from your body.

  Protects your body. Qi guards against invasion of external causes and protects against internal causes.
- Maintains all organs, blood and bodily fluids within the physical systems to which they belong. Qi maintains blood within the circulatory system to prevent hemorrhaging and keeps your internal organs suspended appropriately to prevent them from sagging- for example, a prolapsed uterus.

- Energizes your body- Qi keeps your body energized by maintaining the back-and-forth transformations of Qi and the metabolism of your body.

(G) Classifications of Qi:

- Primordial (Yuan Qi)- The most fundamental and important Qi. It is primarily inherited genetically. It can be strengthened or depleted throughout the course of life. It provides the most important part of vitality. It nourishes and supports all the other specific energetic systems. It dictates growth, development and aging.

- Ancestral (Zong Qi)- Originates from within the region of your chest (lungs and heart) and is closely connected to the air you breathe. Its main function is to support breathing and blood circulation.

- Protective (Wei Qi)- The Qi created from nutrients by spleen energy, supported and enhanced by kidney energy, and distributed by lung energy. It is active and circulates primarily along the exterior of your body to protect against the invasion of external causes.

- Nutritive (Ying Qi)- This is the Qi most intimately associated with the vital substance of blood. It circulates along the blood vessels.

  Its primary function is to deliver nutrients throughout the body.

  Meridian (Jin Qi)- This is the Qi that circulates within the meridians. It connects all the energetic systems and parts of your body into an integrated whole. It nourishes, regulates and detoxifies. This is the Qi that acupuncture primarily works through.

- Organ (Zang fu Qi)- This Qi belongs to and carries the functions of each individual major and minor energetic system. In an occidental sense, this Qi empowers the physiologic functions of each organ.

- Essential Energy (Jing Chi)- This is a potent type of energy derived from the conversion of the purest, most potent forms of essence in the body, particularly sexual fluids, hormones and neurochemicals. When these essential fluids are conserved rather than dissipated, they may be transformed into the more potent energy of jing-chi through the internal alchemy (nei-gung) of the three treasures. This sort of energy suffuses the entire body with a potent vitality that enhances immunity, promotes mental clarity, increases stamina and prolongs life.

- Spiritual energy (Ling-chi)- Is the subtlest and most highly refined of all energies in the human system and the product of the most advanced stages of practice, whereby the ordinary energies of the body are transformed into pure spiritual vitality. This type of highly refined energy enhances spiritual awareness, improves all cerebral functions, and constitutes the basic fuel for the highest level of spiritual work, such as gestating the 'spiritual embryo' of immortality, attaining the enlightened state of mind and achieving the body of pure light known as the 'Rainbow Body', which serves as a vehicle of entry into the astral realms of existence and beyond the material world.

(H) Basic Modes of Moving Energy:

- Shi-chi (drawing energy in): This term refers to methods by which energy is drawn into the system from external sources through vital energy gates on the body. The points most often used for this purpose are the yung-chuan (bubbling spring) points on the soles of the feet, the lao-gung (labor palace) points on the palms of the hands, the ni-wang-gung (medicine palace) bai-hui (hundred confluence) points on the crown of the head, the hui-yin (yin confluence) point at the perineum, and the tan-jing (central terrace) point at the heart. This method requires one-pointed mental focus on the energy gates selected for practice, the visualization of energy as light flowing through the point, and the concerted application of intent to draw energy in through the gates. Energy usually enters the system on the inhalation of breath.

- Shing-chi (circulating chi): This mode is used to circulate energy through the major channels, vital meridians, and minor capillaries of the human energy network. Its purpose is to clear obstructions and eliminate stagnant energy from the channels, irrigate the organs and tissues with fresh energy, balance yin and yang polarity throughout the system and harmonize the vital functions governed by the five elemental energies. It may also be employed to target specific organs or tissues for treatment with healing energy, or to circulate energy in particular channels for refinement and transformation, such as in the microcosmic orbit meditation practice.

- Pai-chi (expelling energy): This method is used to expel stagnant, toxic, excess or other unwanted energies from the system by moving it out through specific energy gates, such as on the palms and soles, and the point between the eyebrows. This sort of energy is usually visualized as dark fog or smoke as it is driven from the system, and it is expelled on the exhalation phase of breath. It may be used to clear the entire system or to purge specific organs via their related meridians and points.

- Huan-chi (exchanging energy): Exchanging energy means intermingling one's energy with an external source in order to refresh, recharge and rebalance one's entire energy system. For example, practicing huan-chi on the beach or high up on the mountains quickly recharges the whole system with the pure, potent energies generated by oceans and mountains. Practicing in a forest allows one to exchange their energies with trees, which produce very potent chi. In dual cultivation style of Taoist sexual yoga, male and female intermingle and exchange their energies in order to boost and balance one another's vitality through the internal alchemy of sexual essence and energy.

- Yang-chi (cultivating energy): This refers to the phase of practice in which internal energy is concentrated and stored in the lower elixir field center below the navel, in other major storage centers or in a specific organ targeted for tonification. For example, you may wish to cultivate wood energy for the liver or water energy for the kidney system or cultivate the essential energy of hormones to boost vitality.

- Lien-chi (refining energy): Refining energy means to increase the purity and potency of a particular type of energy, and this is usually done in still sitting practice, using fusion of mind and breath to refine energy in the 'cauldron' of the lower elixir field, then slowly drawing it upward along the spine into the upper elixir field in the head. This mode of internal practice is often compared with the external alchemy of trying to refine pure gold from baser metals, using the 'fire' of internal heat, the 'water' of vital essence, and the 'wind' of breath in the cauldron of the energy center in the abdomen.

- Hua-chi (transforming energy): Transformation of essence into energy and energy into spirit is one of the fundamental formulas in the internal alchemy of the three treasures of life. The first stage involves the conservation, concentration and purification of vital essence, particularly hormones, sexual fluids and neurotransmitters. These fluids are then 'steamed' in the energy centers in order to transform them into higher forms of energy, the highest form being the ling-chi utilized for advanced spiritual work.

- Fa-chi (emitting energy): This is the mode of energy work used by master chi-gung healers to transmit healing energy from their own energy fields into the systems of their clients. Such energy is almost always emitted from the lao-gung point in the palm of the hand, although sometimes the fingertips, feet, brow point or even the entire body may be used for transmitting healing energy. In China, martial artists sometimes used this technique to deliver an 'energy blow' to vulnerable points on their opponent's bodies, or to envelope themselves in a protective shield of energy to deflect similar blows aimed at them.

(I) Chi-gung: Pillar of Life

Chi-gung is an integral and essential component in the ancient Taoist system of healthcare, life extension and spiritual self-cultivation yang-sheng dao, or the 'Tao of Cultivating Life'. This system is patterned on the eternal ways of nature and the transcendent laws of the universe and includes everything from diet and herbal supplements to breathing and exercise, sexual yoga and chi-gung, meditation and internal alchemy, awareness and attitude. In order to gain full benefit from chi-gung, it must always be properly practiced within the overall context of the whole yang-sheng system of cultivating life.

Of all the various yang-sheng methods of cultivating health and longevity, chi-gung is one of the swiftest and most effective ways to nurture, balance and manage the basic energies of life. As well as working on a physical level in the body, chi-gung enhances cerebral functions and awakens latent talents and abilities that might otherwise lie dormant forever. It also pacifies emotions and balances mood, stimulates the cultivation of the highest spiritual virtues by opening the mind to the universal wisdom of enlightened awareness.

Cultivating spiritual virtues such as wisdom, compassion, patience and tolerance is every bit as important in chi-gung practice as cultivating physical strength, health and power, for without the virtues of spirit, the power of chi-gung is easily bent towards deviant purposes by the fickle fire mind of the human ego and selfish emotions. Using the power and latent abilities awakened by chi-gung for fighting, fortune-telling, gambling and profiteering are typical examples of what can happen when chi-gung is practiced without guidance from the wisdom and intent of spirit. The end result of all deviant applications of chi-gung is the total loss of power, erosion of health, foreshortening of life and ultimate exclusion from the higher realms of existence after death.

The reason for this is quite clear: besides nurturing the energies required for life on earth and promoting longevity of the physical body, chi-gung also opens a gate to the infinite powerful forces of the universe and establishes a direct link between the personal energy field of the individual practitioner and the universal energy fields of the cosmos and all creation. Anyone who tries to harness this power without respecting the wisdom and compassion with which it is inseparably linked at the source of creation is truly 'playing with fire' and is very likely to get badly burned.

In human life, most people enslave their minds and spend their energies to serve their bodies and satisfy their desires, thereby 'mistaking the servant for the master'. In the higher orders of the universe, which human life was designed to reflect, spirit is the master, and energy is the tool through which the spirit expresses its creativity in material form. In order to harness the power of the universe for the benefit of humanity, human beings must pattern their bodies as well as their minds on the universal order of creation reflected in nature and the cosmos known as the Tao, for this is the context in which human life evolved. When practicing the Tao, one must learn to balance physical health and vitality with spiritual awareness and virtue, for that is the one and only way the Tao woks.

(J) Vital Substances

- Blood (Xue)- The primary function of blood is to nourish. Blood is created primarily from nutrients extracted from the food you eat and is converted by spleen energy, transported to lung energy and combined with your primordial Qi, which is then powered in the circulatory system. During this circulation all 5 major energetic systems are involved in maintaining its movement and distribution.

- Fluid (Jin Ye)- Includes all your secretions such as gastric juices, tears, saliva and perspiration. Contains many other substances that are important to your body. Thereby, it also has nourishing properties. The fluid in the body is continuously interconnected with blood. The creation of fluid is initially accomplished through the function of spleen energy. Spleen energy extracts and absorbs fluid from ingestion of water and foods. These absorbed fluids are transported to lung energy, which distributes them throughout your body. During this process kidney energy is involved in fluid regulations and distributions. The small intestines energetic system and the large intestine energetic system are also involved. The small intestine separates the pure fluid from impurities, and the large intestine reabsorbs some fluid. A disharmony of fluids produces visible or invisible phlegm and dampness.

- Essence (Jing)- Essence is entirely inherited, a specific part of kidney energy that governs reproduction and cultivation. Although it is inherited, your Jing can be strengthened or depleted during your lifetime. It is confined within the kidney energy system.

- Shen- In a broad sense, Shen is spirit without an institutional affiliation. For example, an individual who has the presence of good wellness, balance and harmony as well as the radiance of health is acknowledged to "have shen". An oriental physician is trained to observe the patient's Shen. Shen is all of the mental and psychological functions and activities of an individual. In the oriental culture, if your Shen is blurred, it means you are not alert. Generally, the more Shen one has, the more balanced one's body will be. Shen is closely associated with heart and kidney energies. In order for Shen to be created and sustained there needs to be a balance of vital substances: Qi, blood, fluid and essence as well as a balance of kidney and heart energies.

Chapter 4: Yin and Yang: Restoring Balance

Optimal health is achieved through a state of balance and harmony that involves body, mind and environment.

Harmony is determined by the balance between Yin and Yang. Yin and Yang are the most basic concepts used in Eastern philosophy to characterize the world and life. Eastern sages viewed yin and yang as the essence of existence and changes. Everything embodies yin and yang, and the interactions and movement between yin and yang provide a dynamic source for the occurrence, cultivation and shifting of things.

Originally, yang, meaning "the sunny side of the mountain", represented the positive or active aspects. Yin, meaning "the shady side of the mountain", represented the negative or passive aspects. Yang is heat, light, day, summer, vigor, masculinity, upwardness, exterior and function. Yin is cold, dark, night, winter, stillness, femininity, downwardness, interior and substance. A common conceptualization of yin and yang is water(yin) and fire(yang).

(A) Excess and deficiencies

- Physical- Symptoms that are degenerative, recessive, weak and lowering body temp or causing a cold feeling are considered yin. Symptoms that are inflammatory, expressive, agitated and elevating body temp or causing a hot feeling are considered yang.

- Emotional- Depression, sadness, withdrawal and lack of motivation are yin. Anxiety, anger, aggression and mania are yang.

- Personality Traits- Reserved, introverted, calm, steady and reticent are yin. Ostentatious, extroverted, excitable, volatile and outspoken are yang.

- Constitution- A being whose body tends to run on the cool side, who likes to dress warmly and prefers warm weather, has more of a yin constitution. The being whose body tends to run hot, who likes to dress coolly and prefers cool weather has more of a yang constitution.

(B) Major and Minor energetic systems

*5 major energetic systems: yin

- Kidney energy- Provides the most important part of your vitality by storing and generating Jing(essence). Is responsible for sexuality and reproduction, structural integrity and functions of the bones. It also serves a major part of cognitive functions such as memory, concentration and the capacity to process information. Regulates bodily fluids. Dictates growth and cultivation. The fluctuations of the life cycle- conception, birth, adolescence, old age and death- are dictated by kidney energy. It is also responsible for part of the function of breathing, specifically deep breathing. The strength of your kidney energy is reflected in the state of your hair (lustrous vs. dry and brittle). Is particularly connected to the ears, in that many disorders affecting the ears are treated by harmonizing kidney energy. Emotional connections are fear/courage. Kidney energy is associated with the minor energetic system of the urinary bladder. This association determines that the disharmony of each can affect the other systems.

- Heart energy- Provides the main dynamic source for blood circulation. Is closely associated with Shen. Is reflected in the state of your complexion (glowing and vibrant vs. dull and dry). The heart is connected with the tongue, in that many disorders of the heart are reflected in the appearance of the tongue and, conversely, some disorders affecting the tongue are treated by harmonizing heart energy. Emotional connections are happiness/agony. Is associated with the minor energetic system of the small intestine.

- Lung Energy- Responsible for breathing. Is closely associated with Qi, particularly in that Qi connects our body with the environment. Is involved in the distribution of nutrients and fluid and is also part of the regulating process of blood circulation, which is similar to the ideas of modern occidental medical practices. Is reflected in the state of your skin (moist and firm vs. dry and wrinkled). Is particularly connected to the nose, in that the nose is the gateway to the lungs. Many external causes affect the lungs via the nose, and the majority of disorders and symptoms involving the nose are treated by harmonizing lung energy. Emotional connections are sorrow, grieving and chronic worry. Is associated with the minor energetic system of the large intestine.

- Spleen energy- Represents a major part of the digestive function; not just for food but also for fluid assimilation and regulation. It is responsible for providing nourishment for the entire body. It also controls circulation by regulating blood coagulation. Determines the strength of the muscles and functions of the limbs. Is reflected in the state of your lips (moist and plump vs. dry and cracked). The spleen is connected to the mouth, in that many disorders affecting the mouth are treated by harmonizing, spleen energy. Emotional connections are pensiveness and profound or obsessive thoughts. Is associated with the minor energetic system of the stomach.

- Liver energy- The great regulator of our body. It regulates energy flow and circulation, digestion, emotions, fluid and menses. It stores and releases blood. Is reflected in your fingernails and toenails (smooth and strong vs. cracked and brittle). Is connected to the eyes, in that many disorders affecting the eyes are treated by harmonizing liver energy. Determines the strength and flexibility of the body's tendons and ligaments. Emotional connections are anger/sadness. Is associated with the minor energetic system of the gallbladder.

*6 minor energetic systems: yang

- Small intestine- Associated with heart energy, stores and transports foodstuffs and helps to separate the purity (nutrients) from the impurity (digestive waste) within the foodstuffs.
- Gallbladder- Associated with liver energy, stores and releases bile and assists in digestion, which is identical to the contemporary view of its function.
- Urinary Bladder- Associated with kidney energy, it stores and eliminates urine.
- Stomach- Associated with the spleen energy; stores, transports and assists in the digestion of food. After food has left the stomach, stomach energy moves purities downward through the gastrointestinal tract to the small intestines and ultimately the large intestine. As stomach energy pushes downward, the purities are extracted by spleen energy, which moves these purities upward and distributes them to nourish your body.
- Large intestine energy- Associated with lung energy, the main function of large intestine energy is the transportation and elimination of digestive waste.
- San Jiao (triple warmer)- Is not an actual organ-based energetic system, but rather a functionality through which most of the major and minor energetic systems are integrated. Through its functional activity the metabolism of nutrients and fluid is accomplished.

*Overall breakdown of the energetic systems:

I. Kidney

- Associated minor energetic system and function: urinary bladder (stores and transfers urine).
- Main Function: stores and generates Jing (essence); governs development and sexuality; provides vitality; regulates fluid; assists inhalation; nourishes and supports brain and cognitive functions.
- Reflections: bones, ears, genitals/anus, hair, teeth and saliva.
- Dominant emotion: fear and shock.

II. Liver

- Associated minor energetic system and function: gallbladder (stores and releases bile and assists digestion).
- Main function: regulates Qi and blood movements; stores blood; regulates emotions; regulates digestion; regulates menstruation.
- Reflections: tendons/ligaments, eyes, nails and tears.
- Dominant emotions: anger and sadness.

III. Heart

- Associated minor energetic system and function: small intestine (stores and transfers foodstuffs; separates the purity from impurity in foodstuffs).
- Main functions: governs blood circulation and stores Shen (aura).
- Reflections: blood vessels, tongue, facial complexion and sweat.
- Dominant emotions: happiness and joy.

IV. Spleen

- Associated minor energetic system and function: stomach (stores and transfers foods and assists in digestion).
- Main Functions: Governs digestion and assimilation; provides nutrients for body; assists fluid metabolism; contains and prevents bleeding.
- Reflections: muscles, mouth, limbs, lips and gums.
- Dominant emotion: thought and pensiveness.

V. Lungs

- Associated minor energetic system and function: large intestine (transports and eliminates digestive waste).

- Main function: governs breathing; assists Qi generation; supports immune system; assists distribution of nutrients; assists fluid regulation and blood circulation.

- Reflections: skin, nose and mucus.

- Dominant emotions: sadness and grief.

(C) 7 Major (common) Emotions

1. Joy

   - Harmful to corresponding organs: Excessive joy is harmful to the heart for two reasons. First, energy of the heart produces joy. Excessive joy consumes heart energy. Second, excessive joy relaxes the heart to the extent that the heart cannot focus on its activities, which impairs the capacity of the heart to function effectively.

   - Mutual Reduction: Fear and shock overcome joy. It helps to eat more salty foods, which act on the kidney to reinforce fear and shock. Worry and sadness reduce joy also. It helps to eat pungent foods, which act on the lungs to reinforce worry and sadness.

2. Anger

   - Harmful to corresponding organs: Excessive anger is harmful to the liver for two reasons. First, energy of the liver produces anger, and excessive anger consumes liver energy, which leads to deficiency. Second, excessive anger makes liver energy rise to the head, which may cause headaches and impair the capacity of the liver to function effectively.

   - Mutual Reduction: Worry and sadness overcome anger. It helps to eat more pungent foods, which act on the lungs to reinforce worry and sadness. Thought reduces anger as well.

   It helps to eat sweet foods, which act on the spleen to reinforce thought.

3. Worry and Sadness:

   - Harmful to corresponding organs: Excessive worry and sadness are harmful to the lungs for two reasons. First, energy of the lungs produces worry and sadness and excessive worry and sadness consume lung energy quickly, which leads to deficient lung energy. Second, excessive worry and sadness can cause abnormal pain and swelling and impair the capacity of the lungs to function.

- Mutual Reduction: Joy overcomes worry and sadness. It helps to eat more bitter foods, which act on the heart to reinforce joy. Anger reduces worry and sadness. It helps to eat more sour foods, which act on the liver to reinforce anger.

4. Thought

- Harmful to corresponding organs: Excessive thought is harmful to the spleen for two reasons. First, energy of the spleen produces thought, and excessive thought consumes spleen energy, which leads to deficiency. Second, thought causes congestion of spleen energy, which impairs the capacity of the spleen to function effectively.

- Mutual Reduction: Anger overcomes thought. It helps to eat more sour foods, which acts on the liver to produce the needed emotion of anger. Fear and shock reduce the intensity of thought. It helps to eat more salty foods, which act on the kidneys to produce the needed emotions of fear and shock.

5. Fear & Shock

- Harmful to corresponding organs: Excessive fear and shock are harmful to the kidney for two reasons. First, energy of the kidneys produces fear and shock, and excessive fear and shock consume kidney energy, which leads to deficient kidney energy. Second, fear causes kidney energy to move downward, and shock causes a chaotic condition of kidney energy, both of which impair the capacity of the kidneys to function effectively.

- Mutual Reduction: Thought overcomes fear and shock. It helps to eat more sweet foods, which act on the spleen to reinforce thought. Joy reduces fear and shock. It helps to eat more bitter foods to reinforce joy.

(D) Formulas

1) Sour Foods:

- Enhances: liver and gallbladder.
- Stimulates: anger

- Reduces: thought

2) Bitter Foods:

- Enhances: heart and small intestine.
- Enhances: joy
- Reduces: sadness & worry

3) Sweet Foods:

- Enhances: spleen and stomach.
- Stimulates: thought
- Reduces: fear and shock

4) Pungent Foods:

- Enhances: lungs and large intestine.
- Stimulates: worry and sadness
- Reduces: anger

5) Salty Foods:

- Enhances: kidneys and bladder.
- Stimulates: fear & shock
- Reduces: Joy

Chapter 5: Causes of Disease

*(1) external causes, (2) internal causes, (3) non-internal causes, (4) nonexternal

1. External Causes: wind, cold, summer heat, dampness, dryness and fire. External causes do not refer to actual physical entities of wind, cold, heat, dampness, dryness or fire but rather imply that a given cause shares the properties of all these phenomena. In other words, wind does not mean that your body is invaded by a gust of wind. Rather, the cause shows similar properties of those of wind, such as being transient and changeable, appearing and disappearing quickly. Wind,

cold, summer heat, dampness, dryness and fire are symbolic. A disease is typically caused by a combination of several causes.

- Wind: In nature, wind is swift, mobile, changeable and strikes suddenly. Consider the flu, which is often caused by the external cause wind. It invades your system with a sudden onset of illness, and the symptoms can also change rapidly. The condition can begin with a sore throat. By the time you receive medication for your sore throat the symptoms may have moved to your chest.

- Cold: Associated with degeneration and a decrease in metabolism. In nature cold is contracting, congealing, stiffening and tightening. A patient suffering from flu can also suffer from chills, tight muscles and stiff joints.

- Summer Heat: Characterized by a pronounced inflammation, accelerated metabolism and hyperactivity. For instance, a patient with acute pneumonia with high fever, profuse sweating, thirst, dehydration and agitation and even delirium would be said to be suffering from the external cause heat.

- Dampness: Connected with properties such as abnormal accumulation of fluid or moisture, swelling, heaviness, sluggishness and a stubborn and protracted course of illness. Dampness can be seen in the case of fungal or candida infection, or certain dermatological conditions that are characterized by pronounced swelling and oozing caused by an infectious agent, as well as watery diarrhea, edema (water retention) and phlegm accumulation in the lungs or nose.

- Dryness: Mainly damages your body's fluid- such as symptoms that can be seen in certain types of bronchitis where the patient has dry cough, accompanied by pronounced dry mouth, throat, lips and nostrils.

- Fire: Has a property like summer heat, except that it is much more extreme. Many infections are considered to present an element of fire. Fire is present when there is localized swelling, redness and the area is hot to the touch, such as with mumps, and the bodily discharge can become discolored or pustulant.

*Examples of relative proportions:

- Arthritis= external wind= symptoms that are somewhat fleeting and changeable in nature. The pain moves from joint to joint; external cold= significant pain that remains localized in particular joints, and the pain is clearly aggravated by cold environment and/or weather; external dampness= the patient suffers joint swelling and edema; external heat= the patient's arthritis causes notable redness and inflammation.

- The association between external causes and the seasons: external causes are often associated with the seasons. When the energy of the season becomes abnormal or excessive, it can lead to imbalances. For example, wind is predominantly seen in the spring, cold in winter, summer heat and fire in summer, dampness in the late summer and early fall (called long summer in eastern philosophy) and dryness in fall.

- When weather becomes erratic, such as when the temperature becomes unseasonably warm in winter or cold in summer, people's bodies can be thrown out of balance. This abnormal change can cause an incubator effect, providing the invading external cause a highly favorable environment in which to flourish. It is often the case that when there's a sudden cold spell during the summer, there is an outbreak of infectious disease. This is known in Chinese medicine as "untimely energy".

2. Internal Causes: In addition to external, there are also internal causes. These are psychological in nature. The internal causes were described by the Chinese medical classics as the 7 emotions: anger, joy, sadness, grief, pensiveness, fear and shock. These emotions represent a wide range of inner states. They are, by themselves, neither good nor bad. But when excessive or out of control, they can lead to imbalances.

3. Non-internal, non-external causes: Between internal causes and external causes is the third category, called non-internal, non-external causes. This category includes constitutional factors, lifestyle factors, intermediate causes and unforeseen events.

4. Constitutional Factors: Each individual has a unique configuration of yin and yang balance, with a slight tilt one way or another. This defines your energetic individuality. A minor imbalance does not necessarily mean illness. In fact, it is very rare to see a being with a picture-perfect balance. However, a constitutional tendency toward imbalance can interact with an illness, influencing how it manifests and even determining the direction the illness will evolve. For example, when someone with a warm constitution is invaded by a cold cause, although initially

he or she will experience symptoms reflecting the nature of the cold cause, after a short time his or her warm constitution will interact with the nature of the cause, and the being will show signs and symptoms of heat. This is known as the theory of "conformity and transformation", which stipulates how disease and different constitutional types act.

Your unique constitution impacts the way you can get sick. Everyone has their own unique constitution. Some of us run hot, others cold. Some are robust and others delicate. Your constitution will affect the way illnesses develop, progress and resolve.

5. Lifestyle Factors: This includes dietary patterns, stress levels and stress management and excess or indulgence due to lack of moderation and discipline. For example, eating sweets and oily foods tends to generate damp stagnation. Eating overly hot and spicy foods can increase internal heat. Over-eating cooling or cold foods will slow down your energy movement.

6. Intermediate causes: At various stages, some diseases can create or generate disease-causing substances- such as stagnation of blood and phlegm- that cause other illnesses. Others are internal toxins, which are mostly due to abnormally accumulated metabolic waste. Much metabolic waste is toxic to the human body and needs to be regularly eliminated from the body. For example, a patient with severe constipation can have headaches and mood fluctuations due to the reabsorption of toxins simply because the fecal matter stayed inside the body for too long.

7. Unforeseen events: Illness caused by unforeseen events such as accidents and injuries are different from illnesses caused by external or internal factors for obvious reasons, but they can nonetheless cause severe damage to the structure and energy of a healthy being. Therefore, they are considered one of the causes of illnesses and can be treated based on exactly what is damaged.

Chapter 6: Exercise

"Body energy should circulate as regularly and constantly as the Moon and Sun are circulating without a stop."- Dao Shu

It's important to your health to lead an active life. The ancient Chinese put great emphasis on the importance of exercising the body for longevity. A 16th century Chinese physician named Li Ting said, "Everyone knows that prolonged walking and standing can cause excessive fatigue, which is harmful to good health, but few people mention the harmful effects of lying or sitting all day." The Chinese use the term "people of fatigued mind" for people who are constantly consuming their physical energy. The "people of fatigued mind", such as scholars, scientists, authors, and white-collar workers, should take steps to tire their bodies in order to strike a balance between mind and body. The "people of fatigued body", such as farmers, laborers, and blue-collar workers, should take steps to tire their minds in order to achieve mind-body balance.

(A) Walking

The simplest form of exercise in traditional Chinese medicine. It is suitable for all longevity seekers and is a must for older people. Jogging is not recommended exercise in TCM, but walking, which the Chinese call "relaxed steps", is considered very important for good health. Unlike jogging, which is intended to tire the body, walking is intended to relax both the body and the mind.

How is walking conducive to human health and longevity? The Chinese believe that walking can regulate energy and blood circulation as well as relieve the mind and body from fatigue. Walking involves bones, muscles, tendons, and blood vessels throughout the body; walking also provides healthy stimulation of internal organs and the brain and regulates the metabolism.

Specific Benefits:

1. Provides an indirect massage of the internal organs. While you are walking, muscular contractions occur more often and blood circulation speeds up, in effect massaging the heart indirectly and preventing a decline in the heart's energy. No wonder some scientists believe that walking is the best "heart tonic." Walking can also improve the function of the respiratory system because physical activity requires a greater amount of oxygen to perform.

    The action of the lungs is believed to double when walking compared to when you remain inactive.

2. Regulates the metabolism. It has been found that the metabolic rate will increase 15-85% while a man is walking at a speed of about 50 yards or 160 feet per hour, and it increases by 9x when the walking speed doubles. Some metabolic diseases such as diabetes can be prevented simply by walking daily.

3. Walking contains a secret formula for yin tonic. When you feel uneasy, nervous, or tense, your body is shifting toward the yang side, and walking can bring it back to the yin side and strike a balance between yin and yang. In modern medical terms, walking can reduce muscular tension and relax the nervous system to calm you down. Small wonder that some doctors say walking is the best medicine for nervousness and tension.

4. Walking is a source of inspiration. Walking improves blood circulation, which is good for inspiration/insight, because when blood circulation is just right, you can think more clearly and effectively.

(B) Stretching: Benefits and function

Benefits and function

Stretching is very important for flexibility, range of motion and injury prevention. Incorporating stretching into your daily workouts is a given but including it in your day routine is just as important to health and body functioning as regular exercise. It relaxes your muscles and increases blood flow and nutrients to your cartilage and muscles.

- Encourages an optimistic outlook- a buildup of stress causes your muscles to contract, making you feel tense and uneasy. This tension can lead to having a negative impact on mind as well as your body. Stretching exercises have powerful stress-busting abilities. Stretching soon after waking up can help jump-start the mind and body. Stretching loosens tight muscles which helps your muscles both relax and increase blood flow. It is also encouraging the release of endorphins, providing a sense of tranquility and euphoria. Stretching directly before bed will even give you a more comfortable resting experience.

- Fortifies posture- stretching helps ensure correct posture by lengthening tight muscles that pull areas of the body away from their intended position and keeping your muscles loose. Stretching the muscles of the lower back, chest and shoulders can help keep the spine in better alignment and improve overall posture by relieving aches and pains. With reduced pain, there is a reduced desire to hunch or slouch.

- Enables flexibility- the most established and obvious benefit of stretching is improving flexibility and range of motion. An effective flexibility training program can improve your physical performance and help reduce your risk of injury. By improving your range of motion, your body requires less energy to make the same movements and you also will have more flexible joints thus lessening the likelihood of injuries acquired during workouts or during daily activities.

- Increases stamina- stretching loosens your muscles which relieves muscle fatigue and increases blood flow. The longer you exercise the more energy you burn, typically causing one to grow fatigued. With stretching, you can delay the onset of muscle fatigue by ensuring oxygen is effectively flowing through your blood, thereby increasing your endurance.

- Decreases risk of injury- it will help to supply a greater nutrient supply to muscles, thereby reducing muscle soreness and helping to speed recovery from muscle and joint injuries.

  - Improve energy levels- sometimes you may have trouble staying awake during your long, dragging day. If you're feeling this way then it might help to get out of your seat and do a few good stretches for a boost of energy, helping your mind and body to be more alert. Muscles tighten when we get tired and that makes us feel even more lethargic, so feel free to stand up and do some stretches. It will help you to quickly and effectively revitalize your energy levels.

- Promotes blood circulation- it increases blood flow to the muscles. Not only will this help reduce post-workout soreness and shorten recovery time, but it will improve overall health. Greater blood circulation helps promote cell growth and organ function. The heart rate will also lower since it doesn't have to work as hard and blood pressure will become more even and consistent.

- Improve athletic performance- if your muscles are already contracted because you haven't stretched, then they will be less effective during exercise. Regular stretching will relax all your muscles and therefore enable them to be more available during exercise.

- Reduced soreness- stretching before and after a workout gives your muscles time to relax. Increased blood flow increases the nutrient supply to the muscles and relieves soreness in the muscles after a workout.

- Reduces cholesterol- paired with a healthy diet, engaging in prolonged stretching exercises can help reduce cholesterol in the body. This could prevent and even reverse the hardening of arteries, helping one avoid heart diseases.

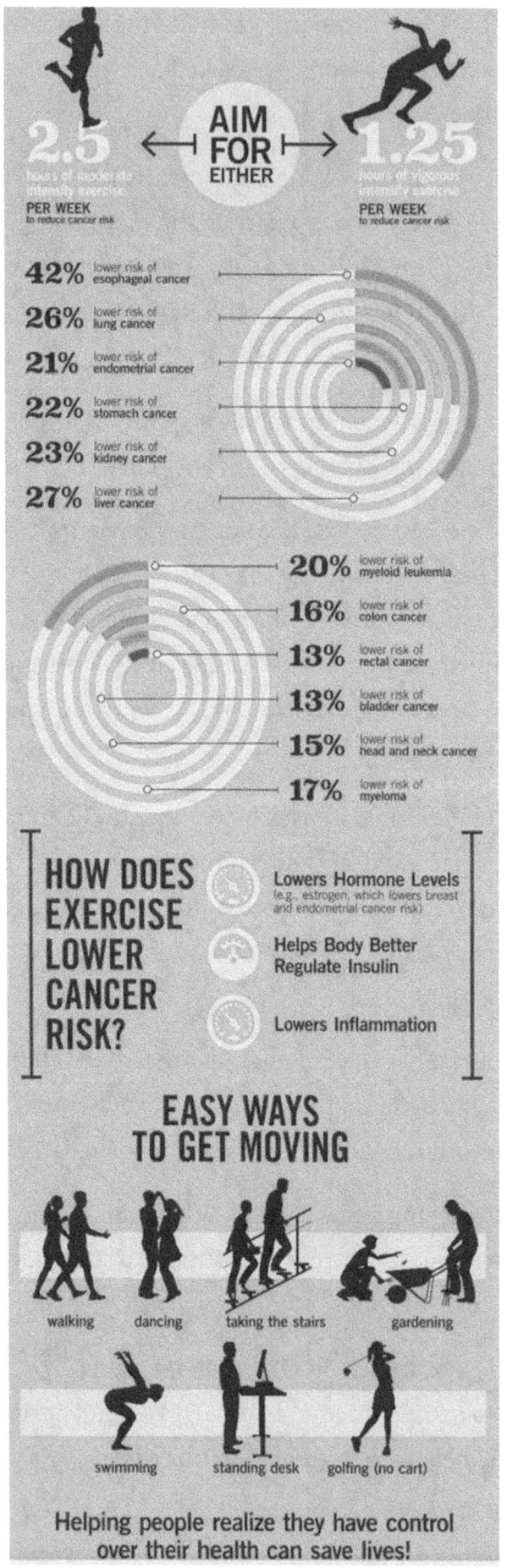

Chapter 7: Meditation: 100 benefits

*Physiological:

- Lower oxygen consumption
- Decrease respiratory rate
- Increase blood flow and slow heart rate
- Increase exercise tolerance
- Leads to a deeper level of physical relaxation
- Good for one with high blood pressure
- Reduces anxiety attacks by lowering blood lactate levels
- Decreases muscle tension
- Helps in chronic diseases like allergies, arthritis, etc.
- Reduces pre-menstrual syndrome symptoms
- Helps in post-operative healing
- Enhances the immune system
- Reduces anxiety
- Enhances energy, strength and vigor
- Helps with weight loss
- Reduction of free radicals
- Higher skin resistance
- Drop in cholesterol levels lowering risk of cardiovascular disease
- Improved flow of air to the lungs; easier breathing
- Decreases aging process
- Higher levels of DHEAS (dehydroepiandrosterone)

- Prevented, slowed or controlled pain of chronic diseases
- Sweat less
- Cure headaches and migraines
- Greater orderliness of brain function
- Less energy wasted
- More inclined to be active
- Significant relief from asthma
- Reduced need for medical care
- Improved athletic performance
- Normalizes you to ideal weight
- Harmonizes our endocrine system
- Relaxes our nervous system
- Produces lasting benefits in changing and/or enhancing brain electrical activity
- Cure infertility (the stresses of infertility can interfere with the release of hormones that regulate ovulation)

*Psychological:
- Builds self-confidence
- Increases serotonin levels, influences mood and behavior
- Resolve phobias and fears
- Helps control own thoughts
- Helps with focus and concentration
- Increases creativity
- Increased brain wave coherence
- Improved learning ability and memory

- Increased feelings of vitality and rejuvenation
- Increased emotional stability
- Improved relations
- Mind ages at slower rate
- Develops intuition
- Increased productivity
    - Improved relationships at home and workAble to see the bigger picture
    - Helps ignore petty issues
    - Increased ability to solve complex problems
- Purifies your character
- Cultivate willpower
- Greater communication between the 2 brain hemispheres
- Better reaction time
- Increases one's perceptual ability and motor performance
- Higher intelligence growth rate
- Increased Job satisfaction
- Increase in the capacity for intimacy
- Decrease in potential for mental illness
- Better, more sociable behavior
- Less aggressive
- Helps in getting rid of addictions
- Reduces pharmaceutical dependency
- Need less sleep to recover from sleep deprivation

- Require less time to fall asleep, helps cure insomnia
- Increases sense of responsibility
- Reduces road rage
- Decrease in restless thinking
- Decreased tendency to worry
- Increased listening skills and empathy
- Helps make more accurate judgments
- Greater tolerance
- Gives composure
- Grows a stable, more balanced personality
- Cultivates emotional maturity

*Spiritual:
- Helps keep things in perspective
- Provides peace of mind, happiness
- Helps you discover your purpose
- Increased self-actualization
- Increased compassion
- Growing wisdom deeper innerstanding of self & others
- Bring body, mind and spirit in harmony
- Deeper level of spiritual relaxation
- Increased self-acceptance
- Helps learn forgiveness

- Changes attitude toward life
- Creates a deeper relationship with your God (higher self)
- Attain enlightenment
- Greater directedness
- Helps living in the present moment
- Creates a widening, deepening capacity for love
- Discovery of power and consciousness beyond the ego
- Experience an inner sense of "assurance or knowingness"
- Increase the synchronicity in your life

*The Holy Spirit (breath):

Breath is the physical counter part of the mind. The mind uses the cerebral cortex of the brain, the twin hemispheres, as its tool. These two hemispheres coordinate with the entire organism through neuromotor responses. All neuromotor activities, all sensory and motor functions of the body, are performed with the help of the breath. So, breath is the mind in action! Breath provides the pranic force to the organism. This pranic force, working as the air element, creates movement, pulsation, vibration, and life. The word "spirit" comes from the Moorish-Latin word spiritus, which literally means breath.

Mind and consciousness are abstract terms--- whereas breath is a physiological reality. The study of consciousness begins with the study of the true science of breathing. Breath induces movement. Breathing itself is a neuromotor activity. The science of controlling prana is known as pranayama, a branch of Hatha Yoga. The term yoga, which literally means "union", refers to a discipline, a way of evolving the higher faculties of mind. There are many paths in yoga, but in essence they all have one purpose--- the union of the self with Th Creator. On a physical level, this means the union of the lower brain with the upper brain. Man's faculties of abstract thinking and aspirations for the higher ideals of life (seated in the cerebral cortex) often conflict with his instinctive, animal nature (seated in the lower brain). Through yoga, man can learn to master his lower brain and pursue higher ideals, to act in accord with the law of universal good. While his animalistic nature makes man hedonistic and selfish, yogic training makes him selfless.

Nostrils and the brain:

Each nostril, when it operates independently, influences the body chemistry in a different way. When both nostrils operate simultaneously, the body chemistry alters so as to make meditation rather than worldly activity appropriate to engage in. The right nostril, being solar or heating in character, increases acidic secretions, whereas the left nostril, being lunar or cooling, increases alkaline secretions. Both right and left nostrils are connected with the opposite sides of the cerebral hemispheres and the olfactory lobe. Since the alternation of breath from one nostril to the other is regulated directly by opposing sympathetic and parasympathetic commands, it is possible that the hypothalamus is the center of the mental processes and behavior in humans. The nose is in direct contact with the hypothalamus by its link with the olfactory lobe of the brain. The hypothalamus regulates body temperature, which influences the mental processes that are interpreted by the brain as emotional states. The hypothalamus is a part of the limbic system—that part of the brain associated with emotions and motivation.

Nostrils, by means of the process of respiration, are connected with neuromotor responses and thus with the autonomic nervous system (sympathetic and parasympathetic). These neuromotor responses influence the hemispheres of the brain and the primary activity of the brain, which is chemical. Neurotransmitters are the brain's chemical messengers; they influence all body functions, including temperature, blood pressure, hormone levels, and regular circadian rhythms.

Nature of the Nostrils:
Through a network of sensory nerves in the nose, the nostrils are connected to subtle nerves, or nadis. These nadis are of two kinds:
1. Conduits of pranic force—*pranavaha nadi*
2. Conduits of psychic energy—*manovaha nadi*

Some of the most important nadis carry both pranic energy (flowing as electromagnetic currents) and psychic energy (flowing as feeling, vibrations, frequencies, etc.) at the same time.

Yogic texts mention fourteen important nadis that carry both kinds of energy. Three of these fourteen are of vital importance. These three nadis: Ida, Pingala and Sushumna, are connected with the limbic system. Activating Ida influences the hypothalamus and the pituitary gland, and thus the growth hormones and anabolic processes; activating Pingala influences the thalamus and hypothalamus but not the pituitary. The Sushumna is connected with the corpus callosum and the cerebellum. When it bifurcates in the brain stem, one branch of the Sushumna goes to the corpus callosum, while the other, known as the posterior Sushumna, passes through the cerebellum to the cerebral cortex and terminates in the corpus callosum. Here it joins the other branch, known as the anterior Sushumna. This point of termination is called the fontanella (the "soft spot" in an infant's skull that hardens after three to six months). Through their connection with the endocrine glands, these three nadis influence body chemistry and the chemical nature of the human organism. The Sushumna nadi is the only nadi that directly pierces all the chakras or psychic centers of the subtle body. These centers are connected with internal organs through sympathetic and parasympathetic nerves, which are connected with the autonomic nervous system working through the spinal column. The Sushumna is thus connected with the network of sympathetic and parasympathetic nerves and the autonomic nervous system through its connection to the chakras and its passage through the spinal column. Although the three nadis meet at the same place in the pelvic plexus, they originate in different parts of the *Muladhara,* or the base of the spine.

Ida and Pingala are located on the left and right side of the spine respectively, but when they are activated, through yogic breathing (pranayama) and the movement of the activated spiritual energy or Kundalini, they crisscross as they move and work on the first five chakras. While the Sushumna terminates in the crown chakra or Sahasrara, the Ida and Pingala nadis terminate in the left and right nostril respectively. The passage of the Sushumna opens only with awakening of the Kundalini which, when dormant, resides in the Muladhara or root chakra. Once activated, this Kundalini energy travels up the body through a very fine channel called *brahmanadi,* located within the Sushumna.

1. **Ida:** This nadi originates at the base of the spine (Muladhara) and works as the left channel. It flows on the left side of the spinal column and terminates in the left nostril by branching into fine capillaries. This nadi becomes active when breathing is carried out by the left nostril. Since Ida is considered to be nourishing and purifying, its energy is called feminine or maternal. The left nostril is connected with the right cerebral hemisphere, making it emotional and magnetic in nature. Because of its dominance during the ascending cycle of the Moon, it is called lunar. The breath flowing through the left nostril is called Ida, or Moon breath.

2. **Pingala:** This nadi originates at the base of the spine and acts as the right channel. It is situated on the right side of the spinal column and terminates in the right nostril, also by branching into fine capillaries. During the operation of the right nostril this nadi becomes active. It is connected with solar currents and its energy is considered to be masculine. The right nostril is connected with the left cerebral hemisphere, making it verbal and rational in nature. Because *it is* dominant during the descending cycle of the Moon, it is called solar. The breath flowing through the right nostril is called Pingala, or Sun breath.

3. **Sushumna:** This nadi originates at the base of the spine and is situated between the Ida and Pingala. It is also known as the central canal or the royal way. Its energy flows through the interior of the spinal column. It pierces the palate at the base of the skull and terminates at the top of the skull.

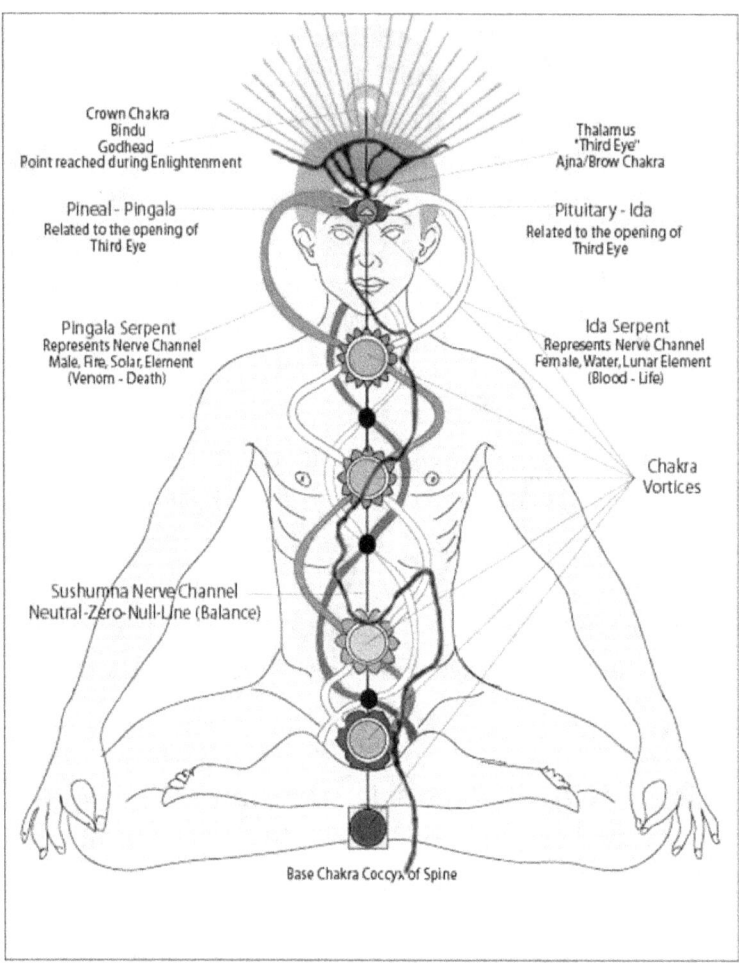

When air flows in both nostrils equally, the Sushumna nadi becomes active. It is fiery in nature. This nadi usually works at dawn or dusk automatically and also, for short intervals, when the transition from one nostril to the other nostril takes place. All human beings breathe through both nostrils just before death, when Sushumna becomes active.

Thus, we see the nostrils are named after their relationship with the solar and lunar currents, which are respectively heating and cooling in nature. Through the periodic alternation of the nostrils the chemical balance is maintained within the organism.

The relationship between the nostrils and the lunar cycles has not yet been discovered by Western neurophysiologists. However, Swara Yoga, as documented by the scripture *Shiva Swarodaya,* has known about this relationship since ancient times. These yogis have clearly stated:

1. The right nostril, which is masculine and connected with the left hemisphere, is associated with the solar planets: The Sun, Mars, and Saturn. On the days corresponding to these planets—Sunday, Tuesday and Saturday—the right nostril works for one hour, starting ninety minutes before sunrise. Half an hour before sunrise, it changes, and the nostril of the day takes over. When the right nostril is also the nostril of the day, flow of breath through this nostril on these three days is auspicious.

2. The left nostril, which is feminine and connected with the right hemisphere, is associated with the lunar planets: The Moon, Mercury, Jupiter and Venus. Every Monday, Wednesday, Thursday, and Friday the left nostril works for one hour, starting ninety minutes before sunrise. Half an hour before sunrise, the nostril of the day takes over. When the left nostril is also the nostril of the day, flow of breath through this nostril on these four days is auspicious.

3. The Sushumna nadi is active when both nostrils function together. It automatically operates very briefly at dawn or dusk, when the nostril connected with the planet (as described above) stops and the nostril of the day takes over. This nadi is not influenced by either the ascending or descending cycles of the moon.

The Nostrils and Special Activities:

By direct observation, the Swara yogis discovered the link between breath and the efficient performance of specific activities. Their findings correspond to the observations of contemporary neurobiologists who have discovered that changes in cerebral dominance occasionally occur prior to changes in nostril dominance. Both ancient and modern scientists corroborate: the right side of the body is connected with the left hemisphere of the brain and vice versa. Breath directly influences the peripheral autonomic nervous function. Breathing through the left nostril definitely influences the cortical activity on the right side of the brain more than the left, and vice versa. In the words of Dr. Khalsa, "Right nostril/left hemisphere dominance corresponds to phases of increased activity. Left nostril/right hemisphere dominance represents the rest phase."

As mentioned earlier, breath is connected with the mind, which uses the brain as its tool. The twin hemispheres of the brain are tools of the mind, each with specific, highly specialized functions (although they do share some activities). This specialization is called lateralization of activity in the hemispheres. Localization of function, which is asymmetrical, makes the hemispheres have separate cognitive strategies. However, the brain-mind functions in a holographic manner to synthesize and integrate sensate responses, thinking, and higher intuition (perception) into a multidimensional awareness.

Under the dominance of different hemispheres, a person will handle the same situation in a different manner. The nostrils serve as indicators of cerebral dominance and may help the person anticipate his or her response to given circumstances. If one understands this point and performs those actions that are best suited for the hemisphere that is dominant at that moment, one can make the best use of his or her energy.

Qualities Associated with the Nostrils:

LEFT NOSTRIL	RIGHT NOSTRIL
- Days: Monday, Wednesday, Thursday, And Friday - Cycle: Ascending Moon Cycle - Directions: (to be avoided for travel): East and North - Influential Levels: Ahead, left, above - Nature: Magnetic, feminine, lunar, alkaline - Suitable for: Peaceful activities - Duration: One to two hours - Connected with: Right hemisphere of the brain; left side of the body - Dominant: Morning following new moon night - Sanskrit Name: Ida - Body Chemistry: Mucus	- *Days:* Sunday, Tuesday, Saturday - *Cycle:* Descending Moon Cycle - *Directions* (to be avoided for travel): West and South - *Influential levels:* Behind, right, below - *Nature:* Electrical, masculine, solar, acidic - *Suitable for:* Difficult activities - *Duration:* One to two hours - *Connected with:* Left hemisphere of the brain; right side of the body - *Dominant:* Morning following full moon night - *Sanskrit Name:* Pingala - *Body Chemistry:* Bile

Activities Associated with the Nostrils:

LEFT NOSTRIL	RIGHT NOSTRIL
1. Stable business, requiring no movement 2. Long-term activities 3. Journey to a far-off place	1. Unstable business, requiring movement 2. Temporary activities or jobs that can be accomplished quickly 3. Journey to a near place 4. Return journey 5. Studying or teaching martial arts

4. Collection of ornaments 5. Collecting food grains and necessities of life 6. Beginning of study (regular school education) 7. Playing musical instrument 8. Singing 9. Learning to dance 10. Construction of hermitage, temple 11. Planting, gardening 12. Building wells, swimming pools, ponds 13. Giving charity, lending money 14. Marriage; birth of baby 15. Purchasing clothes, ornaments, and land 16. Performing rituals for pacification, appeasement, and attaining worldly prosperity 17. Friendship; meeting relatives 18. Making efforts to establish peace 19. Preparing divine medicine or chemicals; practice of alchemy 20. Treatment of diseases, therapy 21. Worshiping of the Guru 22. Entering a newly constructed house, village, town, new country 23. Thinking about relative's ill health 24. Being initiated into a spiritual order; practicing disciplines	6. Studying hard skills and destructive sciences 7. Writing manuscripts 8. Practice of Shastras 9. Practice of Tantra (yantra and mantra) 10. Destruction of country 11. Chopping wood, lighting a fire 12. Cutting gems and jewels, sculpting, carpentry 13. Accepting charity, borrowing 14. Prostitution, sexual indulgence (for male only) 15. Selling cattle 16. Committing crimes; corrupt practices 17. Eradicating, poisoning, or subduing enemies 18. Hunting, killing; holding a sword 19. Practicing medicine 20. Fighting, dueling, wrestling, boxing 21. Seeing a king, meeting and addressing officials 22. Driving a vehicle 23. Having a discussion or debate 24. Climbing a mountain 25. Invoking and mastering evil spirits; pacifying poison 26. Ordering, giving commands 27. Gambling 28. Swimming across a torrential river 29. Worshiping evil spirits, mastering mantra for power, vigor and bravery 30. Knowledge of unseen and unheard things 31. Purification by vomiting, enema, throat cleansing, water purification of the lower intestinal tract, sinus cleansing, Hatha Yoga exercise, *Kapal Bhati* 32. Using drugs and poisons 33. Taming or riding a four-legged animal

25. Addressing one's master 26. Service 27. Performing auspicious acts 28. Starting a new colony, order, or community 29. Opening a bank account 30. Knowledge of past, present and future 31. Curing fever 32. Applying sandalwood paste to the forehead 33. Tying a four-legged animal 34. Taking a new vow 35. Drinking non-alcoholic beverages 36. Urinating 37. Meditating	34. Drinking liquor 35. Eating and defecating 36. Bathing 37. Captivating members of the opposite sex (for male only) 38. Expressing anger 39. Producing works of illumination 40. Working with accounts, counting, preparing ledgers

Behavior Associated with Right and Left Hemispheres:

LEFT HEMISPHERE	RIGHT HEMISPHERE
• Speech, writing, and abstract power of conversation increases; vocabulary becomes richer and more varied • Likes discussions • Answers questions in a more detailed, extensive manner • Becomes excessively talkative • Becomes more receptive to what others say • Is untouched by intonations of sound or emotions behind sounds • Is unable to distinguish between male and female sounds • Is unable to pair patterns • Powers to grasp or recognize lessen • Imagination and perception becomes defective	• Nonverbal memory, emotional thinking and concrete thinking • Sharply diminished capacity for speech • Difficulty in recalling names of objects in daily use, although the objects are recognized • Uses short, simple sentences • Speech activity is reduced • Answers are given by mime and gestures instead of words • Difficulty in conversing • Silence and inattentiveness to speech • Hearing of loud sounds only; distinction between moods and intonations remains • Can distinguish between male and female sounds

<ul><li>Long-term memory remains</li><li>Short-term memory decreases</li><li>Is unable to recognize winter and summer</li><li>Visual disturbance</li><li>Is easygoing, sociable, cheerful, optimistic</li></ul>	<ul><li>Nonverbal sounds are heard; recognizes tones and tunes but not words</li><li>Deterioration in verbal perception and selective improvement in all aspects of imaginal</li><li>perception</li><li>Can easily select pairs of colors; is quick to evaluate unfinished drawings and identify defects</li><li>Loss of theoretical knowledge (schooling)</li><li>Shapes and figures remain in harmony</li><li>Loss of space orientation</li><li>Loss of time orientation</li><li>Is morose, pessimistic</li></ul>

Basic Breathing Techniques:

Respiration is the most important function of the body. It is the source of all energy and life to the being, just as the mainspring is to a clock. Yet most people are not aware of the simple fact that the breath does not flow equally through the two nostrils. At times one nostril is more active than the other, and at other times it may become more dormant than the other. This is because within the nose, on each side of the septum separating the two nostrils, there are structures called turbinates that regulate the pathway of the air within the inner nose. These turbinates are covered by mucus membrane and this membrane is composed of erectile tissue. The swelling of the turbinates changes the inner configuration of the air pathways, and it can thus block or restrict the flow of air. This explains the unequal flow of air through the nostrils. One of the aims of yogic breathing techniques is to equalize this flow, for such equalization is preliminary to the vitalization of the ida and pingala nadis and the opening of the blocked sushumna nadi. Equalizing the flow of breath calms the mind, and in states of deep meditation the equal flow of breath through both nostrils is evident.

Rhythmic Diaphragmatic Breathing:

The most important aspect of breathing is diaphragmatic breathing. The average person uses his chest muscles rather than his diaphragm when he breaths, and such breathing is usually shallow, rapid and irregular. As a consequence, the lower lobes of the lungs, which receive an abundant supply of blood, are not adequately ventilated, and the gas exchange which takes place between the air in the lungs and the blood is inadequate. Respiratory physiologists refer to this as a ventilation- perfusion abnormality. With diaphragmatic breathing such inequalities between ventilation and perfusion are minimized. There is also evidence to suggest that diaphragmatic is beneficial because it increases the suction pressure created in the thoracic cavity and improves the venous return of blood, thereby reducing the load on the heart and enhancing circulatory function.

Though chest breathing has now become natural and involuntary for most of us, it is really a part of the fight /flight syndrome, aroused when the organism is challenged by some external stress or danger. Because of the reciprocity between breath and mind, chest breathing, the breath is shallow, jerky and unsteady, resulting in similar unsteadiness of the mind. All techniques aimed at providing relaxation of the body, nerves and mind will be ineffective unless chest breathing is replaced by deep, even and steady diaphragmatic breathing.

Although diaphragmatic breathing is very simple, easy and beneficial, the habit of doing it has to be consciously cultivated before it can become automatic. A simple practice to achieve this is to lie down on your back, with one palm placed on the center of the chest and the other on the lower edge of the rib cage where the abdomen begins. As one inhales, the lower edge of the rib cage should expand, and the abdomen should rise; as one exhales, the opposite should occur; there should be relatively little movement of the upper chest. By practicing diaphragmatic breathing, one finds in due time that this exercise is becoming habitual and automatic.

Next one should cultivate the habit of harmonious, rhythmic breathing (observing the rate of breath per minute on both inhalation and exhalation is highly therapeutic and is not at all difficult). Breathing between 16-20 breaths per minute is considered average, but when both inhalation and exhalation become slower and smoother, breathing becomes very easy. The student should learn to slow down inhalation first because inhalation is affected by nerve centers, the diaphragm, the intercostal and abdominal muscles. What is more, modern scientists are aware that during inhalation plasma from the capillaries oozes out into the alveolar space (it returns again into the circulation during exhalation). During inhalation nutrients from the blood ooze out into the air sacs (there is an ample supply of enzymes within the sacs to act on the nutrient materials which contain protein, fatty acids and carbohydrates), so lengthening the inspiration increases the time for the metabolic function to take place within the air sacs.

Rhythmic diaphragmatic breathing also brings more air and oxygen into the air sacs of the lungs and into the blood stream. It increases the return of venous blood to the lungs and sends an increased blood supply to the capillaries of the alveoli. It can be practiced in a firm standing position, a steady sitting position, or by lying on your back with the hands along the sides of the body, palms upward, and legs slightly apart (this latter posture is called shavasana, or corpse posture). Exhalation should be through the nostrils, and there should be no external sound. Having exhaled completely, inhalation begins, minimizing the pause, again using the nostrils and making no external sound.

Proper Breathing and its effects on life span:

The nose is the only bodily organ in continuous interplay with the external environment. The rate of our breathing responds quickly to the changes in our physical or mental condition. In anger, for example, breathing becomes fast, and during deep sleep it becomes slow and regular. An average human organism breathes (one inhale and one exhale) 13-15x a minute, which means that our body breathes 21,000 to 21,600x in a 24hour cycle. With an increase in the flow of blood and other vital life fluids. These increases in turn stimulate neuromotor activity that causes the body to utilize more energy. The organism then must convert more oxygen and glucose into energy through internal cellular respiration. These demands do not affect the organism in its growing cycle, but in maturity the organism reacts to wear and tear, the repair mechanism slows down, and the energy level is reduced. The result is increased stress and strain. By maintaining a normal breathing rate of not more than 15 breaths per minute, or by slowing down the breathing rate, we can conserve energy, increase our level of vitality, and live longer.

Breathing affects the whole body:

Breathing is our largest waste removal system. 70% of the waste in our bodies is supposed to be removed via breathing; 20% via skin; and 10% via the kidneys and digestive system.

Few of us breathe deeply enough to oxygenate the blood…. These following breathing vibratory exercises are highly concentrated to drive the oxygen into the blood stream, benefiting the nerve, muscular and glandular systems. Through these exercises you will receive the equivalent of 2 ½ to 3 hours of very active exercises:

- Benefits the heart: close the right nostril. Take a deep breath in through the left nostril. Close both nostrils and hold your breath as long as it is comfortable. Let the breath out through one-half of the right nostril slowly. This is highly concentrated and therefore, is done three times only.

- Benefits the thyroid and parathyroid glands: normalizes weight through correctly balanced metabolism…. It produces thyroxin, which is very important to burn up the toxins (breaking down and building up tissue) and also controls calcium and sex functions. Always sit straight. Using the thumb of the right hand, close the right side of the nose. Take a deep breath in through the left nostril. Close both nostrils for a few seconds, then open the right nostril half-way and let breath out slowly. Now reverse the order-close the left side of the nose, take a deep breath through the right nostril. Close both for a few seconds then open half the left nostril and let the breath out slowly. Do this 10-15x.

- Benefits the lungs: this gets rid of all the stale air in the lungs. Close the right nostril with the right thumb. Take a full deep breath through the left nostril. Close both nostrils expelling breath out through the mouth with a "ha" sound. Alternate this same procedure, first one side then the other 10-15x.

- Benefits the liver and spleen: the liver has over 500 functions in your body…. Take the "r" off and what do you have…. "Live". The liver is the detoxifier in the body. The correct posture is to always sit up straight with no curvature in the spine. Take a deep breath, full breath through the nostrils. Hold your breath. Drop your head back gently. Then bring your head forward exhaling (expelling breath) through the nostrils in a strong manner. Do this 10-15x.

- Relaxation breath: 4-7-8: exhale completely through the mouth, making a whoosh sound. Close your mouth and inhale quietly through your nose to a mental count of 4. Hold your breath for a count of 7. Exhale completely through your mouth, making a whoosh sound to a count of 8. This is one breath. Now inhale again and repeat the cycle three more times for a total of four breaths.

*Pranayama: Activating cranial nerves:

1. Close right nostril. Exhale through left nostril and inhale to a count of 4.
2. Close the left nostril as well and retain the breath to a count of 16.
3. Release the right nostril and exhale fully through it for a count of 8.
4. Keeping the left nostril closed, inhale through the right to a count of 4.
5. Close both nostrils and retain the breath to a count of 16.
6. Release the left nostril and exhale to a count of 8 to complete one round.

*Alternating nostril breathing (pranayama) for a few minutes each day can help to restore balance in the brain, improve rest, calm emotional state, boost your thinking, and relax your nervous system. Most people don't breathe through both nostrils equally. The right nostril symbolizes the Pingala (red, masculine, hot; the sun) and the left nostril symbolizes the Ida (white, feminine, cold; moon). These are the two mythical serpents as seen on the universal symbol for health, the caduceus. They (Ida and Pingala) are two sets of nerves used to transmit the cosmic divine energy of man and are channeled through and stabilized by the sushuma i.e. the spine.

When correct breathing is practiced, the myriad ailments will not occur. When breathing is depressed or strained, all sorts of diseases will arise. Those who wish to nurture their lives must first learn the correct methods of controlling breath thus balancing energy. These breathing methods can cure all ailments great and small.

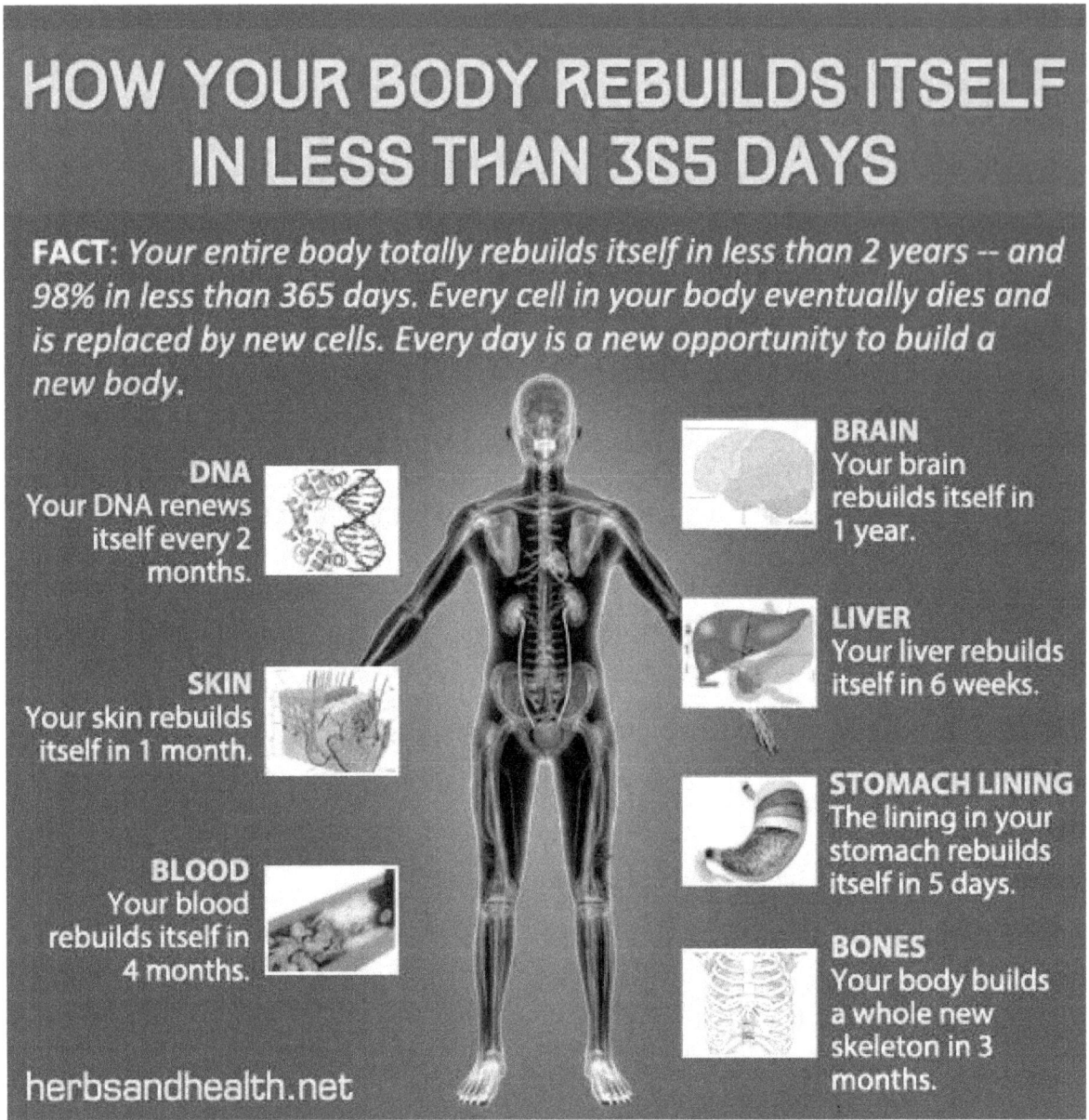

"Keeping your body healthy is an expression of gratitude to the whole cosmos; trees, clouds, everything."- Thich Nhat Hanh

Part 2: Moral Intelligence

"Men and women are to become Godlike through a life of virtue and the cultivation of the spirit through scientific knowledge, practice and bodily discipline."- Ancient Egyptian Proverb

Chapter 1: Science

(A) Knowing Self-7 aspects of study

- Self: is an individual, known or considered as the subject of his or her own consciousness; anything as having and possessing its own personality; personal interests or advantage. Essentially 'self' is anything, any class, or any attribute that, when abstractedly considered, maintains a distinct and characteristic individuality and identity. Apply knowledge one has acquired from study of one's horoscope to refine one's conscious approach to maximizing one's learning and retention capacities. Knowing one's strengths and weaknesses, allows one to take conscious measures of adjustment, for self-improvement and character building.

- Research: is to search into a matter, idea or subject; an investigation which is directed to discovery and analysis of some fact, by careful observation and study of a subject, person, place, thing, or idea; a course of critical or scientific inquiry. The standard of possessing multiple volumes of books in your research efforts, must be maintained and respected; not just for expanded learning, but also for readily available sources for cross-referencing.

- Reflection: is a thought expressed in words; the action of turning (back) or fixing the thoughts on some subject or matter; meditation, and/or deep and serious consideration; the act or business of reflection, with ideas received from sensation and perception. We reflect upon what we study in order to analyze and critique subject matters and disciplines.

- Contemplation: is the action of beholding; the action of viewing; of attentive consideration; of study; and of meditation. Contemplation is an additional (amongst others) study tool. We contemplate upon what we have studied in order to compare, apply reason, and/or to internalize information, considered for validity or invalidity.

- Meditation: is the action, or an act, of meditating; of serious and sustained reflection or of mental contemplation. In religious use, meditation is the continuous application of the mind to the contemplation of some issue or religious truth, mystery, or object of reverence, etc. Meditation improves insight.

- Comprehension: is the grasping of a subject or idea with the mind; and helps one to attain, to accomplish, and to apprehend with the senses. Comprehension means to embrace or to describe summarily. It is the act of comprehending, or a summation of any matter. We test and review our comprehension capacities to measure or judge both our retention of information and the ability to regurgitate the same.

- Analysis: is the resolution of anything complex into its simple elements and reflects the exact determination of its components. It is the resolving of problems, done by reducing them to equations. This may be equated with logistics, also, and involves the process

  of resolving a mathematical problem in its first elements. Thus, analysis is an essential logical synopsis arrived at by reasoning and investigation of the relations of variable elements, components, or the like. This is applied to history or to the examination of an effect, traced to its cause. All the above is applied in critical thinking. Use them!

(B) How to study

1. The spiritual aspirant should read the desired text thoroughly, taking note of any particular teachings which resonates with you.

2. The aspirant should make a habit of collecting those teachings and reading them over frequently. The scriptures should be read and re-read because the subtle levels of the teachings will be increasingly innerstood the more the teachings are reviewed.

3. One useful exercise is to choose some of the most special teachings you would like to focus on and place them in large type or as posters in your living areas so as to be visible to remind you of the teaching.

4. The aspirant should discuss those teachings with others of like mind when possible because this will help to promote greater innerstanding/overstanding and act as an active spiritual practice which the teachings are kept to the forefront of the mind. In this way, the teachings can become an integral part of everyday life and not reserved for a particular time of day or of the week.

5. The study of the wisdom teachings should be a continuous process in which the teachings become the prominent factor of life rather than the useless and often times negative illusory thoughts of spiritual truths. This spiritual discipline should be observed until enlightenment is attained.

(C) Think Before You speak: Process of Elimination

SPEECH FILTERS
THINK BEFORE SPEAKING

FIRST THING THAT COMES TO MIND.

USE JUDGMENT
Do my words need filtering?

INTENTION Am I saying this to hurt the other person?

CHOICE Is this something that I need to say?

COMPASSION Can I understand how the other person feels?

EMPATHY Can I see the other person's point of view?

DID I LISTEN PROPERLY?
Did I give the other person a chance to explain or apologize?

WILL THIS EMBARRASS THE PERSON?
Is there a better way/time/place to say this?

ARE MY WORDS RESPECTFUL?
How would I feel if someone said this to me?

WORD
WORD
WORD
WORD

Chapter 2: Reconnecting the hemispheres

(A) Dimensional Awareness

Something very dramatic happened in the history of our planet.... What happened in the past is now affecting every aspect of our life today.

Everything is connected! There is only one reality and one Creator, but there are many, many ways that the one reality can be interpreted. In fact, the number of ways to interpret the reality are just about infinite. There are certain realities that many people have agreed upon, and these realities are called levels of consciousness.

At one time on Earth we existed in a very high level of awareness that was far beyond anything we can imagine right now.

Because of particular event that happened years ago, humanity fell from that very high place through many dimensions and overtones, ever increasing in density, until we reached this particular place, which we call the third dimension on planet Earth, the modern world.

When we fell- and it was like a fall- we were in an uncontrolled spiral of consciousness moving down through space. When we arrived here in the 3rd dimension, certain specific changes took place, both physiologically and in the way we functioned in reality. The most important change was in the way we breathed prana, a Hindu word for the life-force energy of this universe. Prana is more critical to our survival than air, water or food or any other substance, and the way we take this energy into our bodies radically affects how we perceive this reality.

In Atlantean times and earlier, the way we breathed prana was directly related to the electro-magnetic energy fields that surround our bodies. All the energy forms in our fields are geometric, one of which is a star tetrahedron which is consists of 2 interlocked tetrahedrons. Another way of thinking/visualizing it is as a 3-D star of Daoud (hexalpha; six-point star).

The apex of the upward-pointing tetrahedron terminates one hand length above the head, and the apex of the downward-pointing tetrahedron terminates one hand length below the feet. A connecting tube runs from the upper apex to the lower point through the body's main energy centers, or chakras. This tube, for your body, has the diameter of a circle you make when you touch your longest finger to your thumb. It looks like a glass fluorescent tube, except it has a crystalline structure at the ends that fit into two apexes of the star tetrahedron.

Before our fall, we used to bring prana simultaneously up and down this tube, and the two prana flows would meet inside on of our chakras. Specifically, how and where the prana meets has always been an important aspect of this ancient science, which today is still being studied throughout the universe.

Another major point in the human body is the pineal gland, located almost in the center of the head, which is a huge factor in consciousness. This gland has degenerated from its original size, comparable to a Ping-Pong ball, to its present size, that of a dried pea, because we forgot how to use it a long time ago- and if you don't use it you lose it.

Pranic energy used to flow through the center of the pineal gland. Held inside the pineal gland- even in its shrunken state- are all the sacred geometries and understandings of exactly how the reality was created. It's all there, in every single being. But these innerstandings are not accessible to us now because we lost our memories during the fall, and without our memories we started to breathe differently. Instead of taking in prana through the pineal gland and circulating it up and down our central tube, we started breathing it in through our nose and mouth. This caused the prana to bypass the pineal gland, which resulted in our seeing things in a totally way, through a different interpretation (called good and evil polarity consciousness) of the one reality. The result of the polarity consciousness has us thinking that we're inside a body looking out, somehow separated from what's "out there." This is pure illusion. It feels real, but there is no truth at all to this perception. It's merely the view of reality we have from this fallen state.

For example, there is nothing wrong with anything that happens, for Th Creator is in control of creation. But from one point of view, a polarity view, looking at the planet and how it evolves we should not have fallen here. In a normal curve of evolution, we should not be here. Something happened to us that was not supposed to happen. We went through a mutation- we had chromosome breakage, you might say. So, the Earth has been on red alert for almost 13,000+ years, and many beings and levels of consciousness have been working together to figure out how to get us back onto the path (DNA/RNA) where we were before.

There's another major factor that we're going to focus on…. The geometric energy fields around our bodies can be turned in a particular way, which is also connected to our breath. These used to spin at close to the speed of light around our bodies, but they slowed down after the fall and stopped spinning. When this field is turned back on and spins, it's called mer-ka-ba, and its usefulness in this reality is unparalleled. It gives us an expanded awareness of who we are, connecting us with higher consciousness and restores the memory of the infinite possibilities of our being.

So, the mer-ka-ba is a counter-rotating field of light that affects spirit and body simultaneously. It is a vehicle that can take spirit and body (or one's interpretation of reality) from one dimension or world to another. In fact, the mer-ka-ba is much more than this because it can create reality as well as move through realities. Mer-ka-vah in ibri (Hebrew) means vehicle; that will help us return to our original higher state of consciousness.

To be clear, returning to our original state is a natural process that can be easy or difficult according to our belief patterns. However, simply becoming involved in technical relationships of the mer-ka-ba, such as correcting our breathing patterns or mentally realizing the infinite connections to all patterns of life, for example, is not enough. At least one other factor is even more important than mer-ka-ba itself, and that is the under/inner/overstanding, realizing and living of divine love, sometimes referred to as unconditional love, that is the primary factor that allows the mer-ka-ba to become a living field of light. Without divine love, this machine will have limitations that will never allow the spirit that created it to return home and reach the highest levels of consciousness- the place where there are no levels.

We must be experiencing and expressing unconditional love in order to move beyond a certain dimension.

You (we) presently exist on probably 5 or more levels. Though there is a break between this dimension and others, when you connect with your higher self you mend that break, after which you start becoming aware of the higher levels and the higher levels start paying attention to you- communication begins! This connection to the higher self is probably the most important thing that could happen in your life- more important than understanding any information given. Connecting to the higher self is more important than learning to activate mer-ka-ba, because if you connect to your true self, you will get absolutely clear information on how to proceed step by step through any reality and how to lead yourself back home into the full consciousness of Th

Creator. When you connect with your higher self, the rest will happen automatically. You will still have to live your life, but everything you do will have great power and wisdom within your actions, thoughts and emotions.

When we fell, we divided ourselves into two- really three, but primarily into two- main components, which we call male and female. The right brain, which controls the left side of our body, is our feminine component, though it's truly neither male or female. This is where our psychic and emotional aspect lives. This component knows that there's only one Creator and that oneness is all there is. Though it can't really explain it, it just knows the truth. So, there are not a lot of problems with the female component.

The problem is on the left side of the brain- the male component. Because of the nature of how the male brain is oriented- a mirror image of the female- it has its logical component forward (more dominant), while the female has its logical component toward the back (less dominant). The left brain does not experience oneness when it looks out into the reality; all it sees is division and separation. For that reason, the male aspect of us is having a difficult time down here on Earth. Even our major sacred books such as the Qur'an, the Hebrew and Christian bible have divided, or rather the left-brain dominant thinking and subsequent interpretation thereof, have divided everything into opposites. The left-brain experiences that there is a Creator, but then there's also the devil- perhaps not quite as strong as Th Creator, but a huge influence. So, even Th Creator is seen in terms of duality, as one pole of the opposing forces of dark and light. (This is not true in all sects/aspects of religion.)

Until the left brain is able to see the unity running through everything, to know that there is truly one spirit, one force, one consciousness moving through absolutely everything in existence- until it knows that unity beyond any doubt- then the mind is going to stay separated from itself, from its wholeness and from the fullness of its potential. Even if there's the slightest doubt at all about unity, the left-brain aspect will hold us back, and we can no longer walk on water. Remember, even Thomas walked on water for a short moment when Yeshua asked him to, but one little cell in his big toe said, 'wait a minute, I can't do this', and Thomas sank into the cold water of polarity reality.

There is one and only one image that created all that exists, and that image is the same image that has formed the electromagnetic field around your body. The same geometrics that are in your field can be found around everything- planets and galaxies and atoms and everything else.

It is through balance that spiritual health returns. When the left-brain sees absolute unity, it begins to relax the corpus callosum (the band of fibers joining the two hemispheres) opens in a new way, allowing an integration between the two sides. The link between the left and right brain begin to integrate and synchronize with each other. This action turns on the pineal gland and makes it possible for your meditation to activate the light body of the mer-ka-ba. Then the whole process of regeneration and recovery of our previous higher levels of consciousness can proceed. It is a growth process.

It's the process that's important. Because the process of going from mercury to gold, as symbolized and codified in alchemy, is identical to the process that a human follows going from this level of consciousness into Kerest/Krishna consciousness; there is an exact correlation.

Everything in our world is a waveform or could be even seen as sound. All things- your bodies, planets, absolutely everything- are waveforms. If you choose this particular way of looking at reality and superimpose that view over the reality of the harmonics of music (an aspect of sound), we can begin to talk about different dimensions.

The dimension levels are nothing but differing base-rate wavelengths. The only difference between this dimension and any other is the length of its basic waveform. It's just like a television or radio set. When you turn the dial, you pick up a different wavelength. Then you get a different station on your radio.

It's exactly the same for dimensional levels. If you were to change the wavelength of your consciousness and in so doing, change all your body patterns to a wavelength from this universe.

As you go up into dimensional levels, the wavelength gets shorter and shorter, with higher and higher vibration/energy. As you go down the dimensional scale/levels, the wavelength gets longer and longer, with lower and lower vibration/energy, more and more dense. Just as with a piano, there's a definite place where next note is. In this waveform universe we exist in, there is a very definite place where the next dimensional level exists. It's a specific wavelength relative to this one.

Most beings in the cosmos have this basic understanding/innerstanding of the universe, and they know how to move between dimensions.

Between each whole-note universe and between each subspace or overtone universe, there is nothing- no thing, absolutely zip. Each of these spaces is called a void. The void between each dimension is called the duat by Tamerians/Kamatan (so-called Egyptians) or the bardo by

Tibetans. Each time you pass from one dimension into the next, you pass through the void or darkness that's in between. But certain voids are "darker" than others, and the darkest of these exist between octaves. They're more powerful than the voids that exist within an octave. Please innerstand that these words, though used, cannot fully explain this concept. This void that exists between octaves can be called the great void or the wall. It's like a wall you have to pass through to get to a higher octave. Th Creator put these voids there in a particular way for certain reasons that will soon become apparent.

All of these dimensions are superimposed over each other, and every point in space/time contains them all. The doorway to any of them is anywhere. That makes it convenient- you don't have to go looking for it, you just have to know how to access it. Although there are certain sacred places in the geometries of our reality here on Earth where it's easier to become aware of the various dimensions and overtones- sacred sites, which are nodal points connected to the Earth and the heavens- there are also specific places in space that are tied to the geometries of Earth. These places are sometimes referred to by explorers as stargates, openings to other dimensional levels where it's easier to get through. But in truth, you can be anywhere to go anywhere. It really doesn't matter where you are if you truly innerstand/overstand the dimensions and, of course, are capable of divine love.

We do have free will, and we can change the fate of the world simply through our being.

(B) Wisdom of the East

Everything is vibration, electricity. The body has many different chemicals in its composition. Certain of these chemicals are conveyed to the brain by the blood stream. The brain, you know, has the best supply of blood and its contained chemicals. Those ingredients, potassium, manganese, carbon, and many others, form the brain tissue. Interaction between them makes a peculiar oscillation of molecules which we term an 'electric current.' When one thinks one sets in motion a chain of circumstances which results in the formation of this electric current and, hence, 'brain waves'.

Actually, every being has what we call an individual wavelength, that is, the amount of energy on the basic wave emitted from the brain of any one being follows a precise order of oscillation, and if we could determine the rate of oscillation of the basic brain wave of another being and tune in to that basic oscillation, we should have no difficulty whatsoever in conveying our message by so-called telepathy, irrespective of the distance.

No amount of reading nor looking at pictures will replace practical experience and knowledge.

We give ourselves mental indigestion by reading everything and anything and not absorbing any of it. We imagine that we are great men, men of surpassing spirituality. Instead we are poor blunderers who deceive no one as much as ourselves. We are spiritually bankrupt, knowing all but knowing nothing. The insensate, indiscriminate and ill-advised reading of all that comes one's way is dangerous. Man followed all the great religions and, yet innerstanding none of them, we yet set ourselves up as the greatest spiritual men of all.

The answer is so obvious! Read, read, read, and read again, but never let any book overpower your discrimination or discernment. A book is meant to teach, to instruct or even to amuse. A book is not a master to be followed blindly and without reason. No being possessed of intelligence should ever be enslaved by a book or by the words of another.

Of course, there must be books! The libraries of the world contain most of the knowledge of the world, but no one but an idiot would say that mankind is the slave of books. Books exist merely to be a guide unto mankind, to be a reference, for use. It is indeed a fact that books misused can be a curse, for they lead a man to feel that he is greater than he is and thus lead him to devious paths in life, paths which he has no knowledge of nor the wit to follow to the end.

You cannot go to all the places in the world and study under the greatest masters of the world, but the printed word- books- can bring their teachings to you. You do not have to believe everything you read, nor do the great masters of writing ever tell you that you should, you should use your own judgment and use their words of wisdom as a pointer to what should be your words of wisdom…. A being who is not ready to study a subject can harm themselves immeasurably by getting hold of a book and- as it were- trying to raise themselves above their karmic stations by studying the words and the works of others. It may well be that the reader is a man of low evolutionary development, and in that case, in studying the things which at the present are not for him, he may rather stunt than enhance his spiritual cultivation.

Misuse of occult power or the domination of another being by occult means brings a truly terrible punishment. Esoteric powers, metaphysical powers, and extrasensory perceptions are to be used only for good, only in the service of others, only to increase the sum total of knowledge contained in the world.

Many people read books and try experiments without having a suitable master at hand. Many people get out of themselves, either through drink or through over-excitement or through over-indulgence in something which is not good for the spirit, and then they panic. There is one way in which you can help, throughout your life you should warn those who enquire that the only thing to fear in occult matters is fear. Fear allows undesirable thoughts, undesirable entities to enter and even to take control of one, to take possession of one, and you should repeat again and again that there is naught ever to fear other than fear itself. In casting out fear, then you strengthen humanity and make humanity purer. It is fear which causes wars, fear which makes dissention in the world, fear which turns man's hand against man. Fear, and fear alone, is the enemy, and if we throw out fear once and for all then- believe me- there is nothing more that need be feared.

The things which we are afraid of cannot hurt us unless we permit them to hurt us through our fear.

Fear corrodes the soul. Vain and useless imaginings put one on the wrong path so that with the passage of years realities fade from sight and do not come to light again for several incarnations. Keep your foot on the path, let no wild yearnings nor imaginings color or distort your outlook. This is the world of illusion, but to those of us who can face that knowledge, then the illusion can be turned into reality when we are off this world.

We are entitled to help those who are worthy of help. We are not entitled to help those who do not want our help and are not ready for help. We do not use occult power or ability for self-gain, nor for hire or reward. The whole purpose of occult power is: to speed one's evolution upwards and to help the world as a whole, not just the world of humans, but the world of nature, of animals- everything.

You must practice using the aura and telepathy together. By using one and not the other, your conclusions may be warped. It is essential to use all one's faculties, bring all one's power to bear, on each and every problem.

Illness is merely a dissonance in the body vibrations. An organ has its rate of molecular vibration disturbed and so it is considered to be a sick organ. If we could actually see how much the vibration of an organ departs from the normal, then, by restoring the rate of vibration to what it should be, we have effected a cure. In the case of mental affliction, the brain usually receives messages from the overself which it cannot correctly interpret, and so the actions resulting are those which depart from that which is accepted as normal actions for a human. Thus, if the human is not able to reason or act in a normal manner, he is said to have some mental ailment. By measuring the discrepancy- the under stimulation- we can assist a being to recover normal balance. The vibrations may be lower than normal resulting in under-stimulation, or they may be higher than normal which would give an effect similar to that of a brain fever. Quite definitely illness can be cured by intervention through the aura.

It is clear that those who use sex normally- as it is meant to be used- increase their own spiritual power/force. Sex is not a matter to be abused, but on the other hand nor is it a matter to be repudiated. By bringing vibrations to another being one can increase spirituality. The sexual act should only be indulged in by those who are in love, by those bound together by spiritual affinity. That which is illicit, unlawful, is mere prostitution of the body and can harm one as much as the other can help one. In the same way a male or female should have only one partner, eschewing all temptations which would lead one from the path of truth and righteousness.

For the better type of human or beast it is necessary that the parents shall be fond of each other, that they both be raised in spiritual as well as physical vibrations. Artificial insemination carried out in cold, loveless conditions, results in very poor stock indeed.

Life is like a school. When we are beyond this life in the astral world, before we come down into a woman's womb, we discuss with others what we are going to learn. A being who is going to be born already has everything arranged; the being is going to come down and be born of a certain woman who lives in a certain area and who is married to a certain class of man. It is thought that will give the baby to be born the opportunities for gaining the experience and knowledge previously planned. Eventually, in the fullness of time, the baby is born. First, the baby has to learn to feed, it has to learn to control certain parts of its physical body- it has to learn how to speak and how to listen. At first, you know a baby cannot focus on its eyes, it has to learn how to see. It is at school. None of us like school, some of us have to come, but others of us do not have to come. We plan to come- not for karma- but to learn other things. The baby grows up and becomes a boy/girl then goes to a classroom where often he gets treated rather roughly by their teacher, but there is nothing wrong in that. No one has ever been harmed by discipline. Discipline is the difference between an army and a rabble. You cannot have a cultured man unless that man has been disciplined. Many times, now you will think that you are ill-treated, that the teacher is harsh, and cruel, but- whatever you think now- you particularly arranged to come to this Earth in these conditions.

We come to Earth to learn things, and no matter how hard nor how bitter the lessons which we learn on this Earth, they are lessons for which we have enrolled before we came here. When we leave this Earth, we have our vacation for a time in the other world, and then if we want we make progress and we move on. We may return to this Earth under different conditions, or we may move on to a completely different stage of existence. Often when we are in school we think that there is no end to the day, we think that there is going to be no end to the harshness of the teacher. Life on Earth is like that, if everything went smoothly for us, if we had everything we wanted we should not be learning a lesson, we would just be drifting along on the stream of life. It is a sad fact that we only learn with pain and suffering.

The being has to learn things which are going to be of use in the astral world after leaving the Earth. This is the world of illusion, and it is extremely well suited to teach us hardship and in suffering hardship, we learn to innerstand/overstand the difficulties and the problems of others.

There must be some give and take, because if these people are going to learn anything at all, then they should be sufficiently aware to know that there is something wrong with them.

Every being has a basic frequency of vibration, that is, every being's molecules vibrate at a certain rate and the wavelength generated by a being's brain can fall into special groups. No two beings have the same wavelength- not the same wavelength identical in every respect, but when two people are near the same wavelength, or when their wavelength follows certain octaves of the other, then they are said to be compatible and they usually get on very well together. If a man is to have what is known as inspiration, if he is to be a good artist, this his frequency of vibrations must be many times higher than normal. Sometimes it makes him irritable- difficult to get on with. Being of a higher vibrational rate than most they tend to look down on us lesser mortals. However, often the work that he/she turns out is so good that we can put up with their slight fads and fancies.

Before we came to this Earth, we mapped out what we intended to do. The knowledge was stored in our sub-conscious and if we could get in touch with our sub-conscious- as some can! – then we should know everything we had planned. Of course, if we should know everything that we had planned there would be no merit in striving to be better ourselves because we would know that we know that we were working along a pre-determined plan. For some reason, sometimes a being will go to sleep or will get out of body while conscious and will get in touch with his overself. Sometimes the overself will be able to spring up knowledge from the subconscious and transfer it back to the body on Earth, so that when the astral body returns to the flesh body there is knowledge in the mind of certain things that happened in a past life. It may be a special warning not to commit suicide- as just one example- and if a being has been penalized life after life for doing that, then frequently they will have a memory of something about self-destruction in the hope that such a memory will cause the body to refrain from self-destruction.

To each according to his belief, each according to his needs. The trappings of ceremonial religion are a solace to many, we should not condemn those who have not travelled far enough upon the path, nor are able to stand without crutches.

*Ancillary Wisdom:

- Some secrets are safer kept hidden. Some secrets are too dangerous to share, even with those you love and trust.
- Love is sweet, but it cannot change a man's nature.
- If friends can turn to enemies, enemies can become friends.
- The heart lies and the head plays tricks with us, but the third eye sees true. Look with your inner eye. Hear with your inner ears. Taste with your inner mouth. Smell with your inner nose. Feel with your inner skin. Then comes the thinking, afterward, and in that way knowing the truth.
- Fear cuts deeper than swords.
- In War! Move swift as a deer. Look with your eyes. Move quiet as a shadow. Be as quick as a snake. Be calm as still water. Be as strong as a bear. Be as fierce as a wolverine.
- The man who fears losing has already lost.
- Never do what they expect.
- A man who won't listen can't hear.
- A child sees an obstacle, and runs around it or knocks it down, a man must learn that sometimes words can accomplish what a sword cannot.

Chapter 3: The Art of War

(A) Laying Plans

The Art of War, then, is governed by 5 constant factors, to be considered in one's deliberations, when seeking to determine the conditions obtaining in the field.

These are:

1. Moral Law- causes the people to be in complete accord with their ruler, so that they will follow him regardless of their lives, undismayed by any danger.

2. Heaven- signifies night and day, cold and heat, times and seasons.

3. Earth- comprises distances, great and small, danger and security, open ground and narrow passes; the chances of life and death.

4. The Commander- stands for the virtues of wisdom, sincerity, benevolence, courage and strictness.

5. Method and Discipline- are to be innerstood/overstood as the marshalling of the army in its proper subdivisions, the graduations of rank among the officers, the maintenance of roads by which supplies may reach the army, and the control of military expenditure.

These 5 heads should be familiar to every general: he who knows them will be victorious; he who knows them will not fail.

Therefore, in your deliberations, when seeking to determine the military conditions, let them be made the basis of a comparison, in this wise-

- Which of the two sovereigns is imbued with the moral law?
- Which of the two generals has most ability?
- With whom lie the advantages derived from heaven and earth?
- On which side is discipline most enforced?
- Which army is stronger?
- On which side are officers and men more highly trained?
- In which army is there the greater constancy both in reward and punishment.

(B) Attack by stratagem

Thus, we may know that there are 5 essentials for victory:

- He will win who knows when to fight and when not to fight.

- He will win who knows how to handle both superior and inferior forces.
- He will win whose army is animated by the same spirit throughout all its ranks.
- He will win who, prepared himself, waits to take the enemy unprepared.
- He will win who has military capacity and is not interfered with by the sovereign.

If you know the enemy and know yourself, you need not fear the result of a hundred battles. If you know yourself and not the enemy, for every victory gained you will also suffer a defeat. If you know neither yourself or the enemy, you will succumb in every battle.

(C) Variation in tactics

The art of war teaches us to rely not on the likelihood of the enemy not coming, but on our own readiness to receive him; not on the chance of his not attacking, but rather on the fact that we have made our position unassailable.

There are 5 dangerous faults which may affect a general:

- Recklessness, which leads to destruction;
- Cowardice, which leads to capture;
- A hasty temper, which can be provoked by insults;
- A delicacy of/for honor, which is sensitive to shame;
- Over-solicitude for his men, which exposes him to worry and trouble.

Therefore, the enlightened ruler is heedful, and the good general full of caution. This is the way to keep a country at peace and an army intact.

Chapter 4: King Alfred Plan

(A) Silent weapons for quiet wars

It is patently impossible to discuss social engineering or automation of a society, i.e., the engineering of social automation systems (silent weapons) on a national or worldwide scale without control and destruction of human life, i.e., peonage and genocide.

This manual is in itself an analog declaration of intent. Such a writing must be secured from public scrutiny. Otherwise, it might be recognized as a technically formal declaration of domestic war. Furthermore, whenever any person or group of persons in a position of great power, and without the full knowledge and consent of the public, uses such knowledge and methodology for economic conquest- it must be understood that a state of domestic warfare exists between said person or group of persons and the public.

The solution of today's problems requires an approach which is ruthlessly candid, with no agonizing over religious, moral, or cultural values.

You have qualified for this project because of your ability to look at human society with cold objectivity, and yet analyze and discuss your observations with others of similar intellectual capacity without a loss of discretion or humility.

Such virtues are exercised in your own best interest. Do not deviate from them.

(B) Historical Introduction

Silent weapon technology has evolved from operations research (O.R.), a strategic and tactical methodology developed under the military management in England during world war II. The original purpose of operations research was to study the strategic and tactical problems of air and land defense with the objective use of limited military resources against foreign enemies (i.e., logistics).

It was soon recognized by those in positions of power that the same methods might be useful for totally controlling a society. But better tools were necessary.

Social engineering (the analysis and automation of a society) requires the correlation of great amounts of constantly changing economic information (data), so a high-speed computerized data processing system was necessary which could race ahead of the society and predict when society would arrive for capitulation.

Relay computers were too slow, but the electric computer, invented (uncovered) in 1946, by J. Presper Eckert and John W. Mauchly, filled the bill.

The next breakthrough was the development of the simple method of linear programming in 1947 by the mathematician George B. Dantzig.

Then, in 1948, the 'transistor', invented (uncovered) by J. Bardoen, W.H. Brattain, and W. Shockley, promised great expansion of the computer field by reducing space and power requirements.

With these three in positions of power strongly suspected that it was possible for them to control the whole world with the push of a button.

Immediately, the Rockefeller Foundation got in on the ground floor by making a four-year grant to Harvard college, funding the Harvard economic research project for the study of the American economy. One year later, in 1949, the United States Air Force joined in.

In 1952 the original grant period terminated, and a high-level meeting of the elite was held to determine the next phase of social operations research. The Harvard project had been very fruitful as is borne out by the publication of some of its results in 1953 suggesting the feasibility of economic (social) engineering. (studies in the "Structure of the American economy"-copyright 1953 by Wassily Leontief, international sciences press Inc., White Plains, New York.)

Engineered in the last half decade of the 1940's, the now quiet war machine stood, so to speak, in sparkling gold-plated hardware on the showroom floor, by 1954.

With creation of the Moser in 1954, the promise of unlocking unlimited sources of fusion atomic energy from the heavy hydrogen in sea water and the consequent availability of unlimited social power became a possibility only decades away.

The combination was irresistible. The quiet war was quietly declared by the international elite at a meeting held in 1954. Although the silent weapons system was nearly exposed 13 years later, the evolution of the new weapon system has never suffered any major setbacks.

This volume marks the 25th anniversary of the beginning of the quiet war. Already this domestic war has had many victories on many fronts throughout the world.

(C) Political Introduction

In 1954 it was well recognized by those in positions of authority that it was only a matter of time, only a few decades, before the general public would be able to grasp and upset the cradle of power, for the very elements of the new silent weapon technology were as accessible for a public utopia as they were providing a private utopia.

The issue of primary concern, that of dominance, revolved around the subject of the energy sciences.

(D) Energy

Energy is recognized as the key to all activity on Earth. Natural science is the study of the sources and control of natural energy, and social science, theoretically expressed as economics, is the study of the sources and control of social energy. Both are book-keeping systems: mathematics. Therefore, mathematics is the primary energy science and the bookkeeper can be king if the public can be kept ignorant of the methodology of the book-keeping. All science is a means to an end. The means is knowledge, the end is control. Beyond this remains only one issue, "who will be the beneficiary?"

In 1954 this was the issue of primary concern. Although the so-called "moral issues" were raised, in view of the law of natural selection it was agreed that a nation or world of people who will not use their intelligence are no better than animals who do not have intelligence. Such people are beasts of burden and steaks on the table by choice and consent.

Consequently, in the interest of future world order, peace and tranquility, it was decided to privately wage a quiet war against the

American public with an ultimate objective of permanently shifting the natural and social energy (wealth) of the undisciplined and irresponsible many into the hands of the self-disciplined, responsible, and worthy few.

In order to implement this objective, it was necessary to create, secure, and apply new weapons which, as it turned out, were a class of weapons so subtle and sophisticated in their principle of operation and public appearance as to earn for themselves the name 'silent weapons'.

In conclusion, the objective of economic research, as conducted by the magnates of capital (banking) and the industries of commodities (goods), lands, services, is the establishment of an economy which is totally predictable and manipulatable.

In order to achieve a totally predictable economy, the low-class elements of the society must be; brought under total control, i.e., must be housebroken, trained, and assigned a yoke and long term social duties from a very early age, before they have an opportunity to question the propriety of the matter. In order to achieve such conformity, the lower-class family unit must be disintegrated by a process of increasing preoccupation of the parents and the establishment of government operated day care centers for the occupationally orphaned children.

The quality of education given to the lower-class must be of the poorest sort, so that the meat of ignorance isolating the inferior class from the superior class is and remains incomprehensible to the inferior class. With such an initial handicap, even bright lower-class individuals have little if any hope of extricating themselves from their assigned lot in life. This form of slavery is essential to maintaining some measure of social order, peace, and tranquility for the ruling upper class.

(D) Descriptive introduction of the silent weapon:

Everything that is expected from an ordinary weapon is expected from a silent weapon by its creators, but only in its own manner of functioning.

It shoots situations, instead of bullets; propelled by data processing instead of chemical reaction (explosion); originating from bits of data, instead of grains of gunpowder; from a computer, instead of a gun; operated by a computer programmer, instead of a marksman; under the orders of a banking magnate, instead of a military general.

It makes no obvious, explosive noises, causes no obvious physical or mental injuries, and does not obviously interfere with anyone's daily social life.

Yet it makes an unmistakable 'noise', causes unmistakable physical and mental damage, and unmistakably interferes with daily social life, i.e. unmistakable to the trained observer, one who knows what to look for.

The public cannot comprehend this weapon, and therefore cannot believe that they are being attacked and subdued by a weapon.

The public might instinctively feel that something is wrong, but because of the technical nature of the silent weapon, they cannot express their feelings in a rational way, or handle the problems with intelligence. Therefore, they do not know how to cry for help, and do not know how to associate with others to defend themselves against it.

When a silent weapon is applied gradually to the public, the public adjusts/adapts to its presence and learns to tolerate its encroachment on their lives until the pressure (psychological via economic) becomes too great and they crack up.

Therefore, the silent weapon is a type of biological warfare. It attacks the vitality, options, and mobility of the individuals of a society by knowing, understanding, manipulating, and attacking their sources of natural and social energy, and their physical, mental, and emotional strengths and weaknesses.

(E) Theoretical introduction

"Give me control over a nation's currency, and I care not who makes its laws,"- Mayer Amshel Rothschild (1743-1812)

Today's silent weapons technology is an outgrowth of a simple idea discovered, succinctly expressed, and effectively applied by the quoted Mayer Amshel Rothschild. Rothschild discovered the missing passive component of economic theory known as economic inductance. He, of course, did not think of his discovery in these 20th century terms, and, to be sure, mathematical analysis had to wait for the second industrial revolution, the rise of the theory of mechanics and electronics, and finally, the invention of the electronic computer before it could be effectively applied in the control of the world economy.

(F) General energy concepts

In the study of energy systems, there always appear three elementary concepts. These are potential energy, kinetic energy, and energy dissipation. And corresponding to these concepts, there are three idealized, essentially pure physical counterparts, called passive components.

1. In the science of physical mechanics, the phenomenon of potential energy is associated with a physical property called elasticity or stiffness.

    - In electronic science, potential energy is stored in a capacitor instead of a spring. This property is called capacitance instead of elasticity or stiffness.

2. In the science of physical mechanics, the phenomenon of kinetic energy is associated with a physical property called inertia or mass and can be represented by a mass or a fly wheel in motion.

    - In electronic science, kinetic energy is stored in an inductor (in a magnetic field) instead of a mass. This property is called inductance instead of inertia.

3. In the science of physical mechanics, the phenomenon of energy dissipation is associated with a physical property called friction or resistance and can be represented by a dashpot or other device which converts system energy into heat.

- In electronic science, dissipation of energy is performed by an element called either a resistor or a conductor, the term 'resistor' being the one generally used to express the concept of fiction, and the term 'conductor' being generally used to describe a more ideal device (e.g. wire) employed to convey electric energy efficiently from one location to another. The property of a resistance or conductor is measured as either resistance or conductance reciprocals.

In economics these three energy concepts are associated with:

- Economic capacitance-capital (money, stock/inventory, investments in buildings and durables, etc.)
- Economic conductance-goods (production flow coefficients)
- Economic inductance-services (the influence of the population of industry on output)

All of the mathematical theory developed in the study of one energy system, (e.g., mechanics, electronics, etc.) can be immediately applied in the study of any other energy system (e.g., economics).

(G) Rothschild's energy discovery

What Rothschild had discovered was the basic principle of power influence, and control over people as applied to economics. That principle is "when you assume the appearance of power, people soon give it to you."

Rothschild had discovered that currency or deposit loan accounts and the required appearance of power that could be used to induce people

(inductance, with people corresponding to a magnetic field) into surrendering their real wealth in exchange for a promise of greater wealth (instead of real compensation). They would put up real collateral in exchange for a loan or promissory notes. Rothschild found that he could issue more notes than he had backing for, so long as he had someone's stock of gold as a persuader to show to his customers.

Rothschild loaned his promissory notes to individuals and to governments. These would create over-confidence. Then he would make money scarce, tighten control of the system, and collect the collateral through the obligation of contracts. The cycle was then repeated. These pressures could be used to ignite a war. Then he would control the availability of currency to determine who would win the war. That government which agreed to give him control of its economic system got his support. Collection of debts was guaranteed by economic aid to the enemy of the debt. The profit derived from this economic methodology made Rothschild all the wealthier and all the more able to extend his wealth. He found that the public greed would allow currency to be printed by government order beyond the limits (inflation) of backing in precious metals or the production of goods and services (gross national product, GNP).

(H) Apparent capital as "paper" inductor

In this structure, credit, presented as a pure circuit element called "currency", has the appearance of control, but is, in fact, negative capital. Hence it has the appearance of servive, but is, in fact indebtedness or debt. It is therefore an economic inductance instead of an economic capacitance, and if balanced in no other way, will be balanced by the negation of population (war, genocide). The total goods and services represent real capital called the gross national product, and currency may be printed up to this level and still represents economic capacitance; but currency printed beyond this level is subtractive, represents the introduction of economic inductance, and constitutes notes of indebtedness. War is therefore the balancing of the system by killing the true creditors (the public which we have thought to exchange true value for inflated currency) and falling back on whatever is left of the resources of nature and the regeneration of those resources.

Rothschild had discovered that currency gave him the power to rearrange the economic structure to his own advantage, to shift economic inductance to those economic positions which would encourage the greatest economic instability and oscillation.

The final key to economic control had to wait until there was sufficient data and high-speed computing equipment to keep close watch on the economic oscillations created by price shocking and excess paper energy credits (paper inductance/inflation).

(I) Breakthrough

The aviation field provided the greatest evolution in economic engineering by way of the mathematical theory of shock testing. In this process, a projectile is fired from an airframe on the ground and the impulse of the recoil is monitored by vibration transducers connected to the airframe and wired to chart recorders. By studying the echoes or reflections of the recoil impulse in the airframe, it is possible to discover critical vibrations in the structure of the airframe which either vibrations of the wings or a combination of the two, might reinforce resulting in a resonant self-destruction of the airframe in flight as an aircraft. From the standpoint of engineering, this means that the strengths and weaknesses of the structure of the airframe in terms of vibrational energy can be discovered and manipulated.

(J) Application in economics

To use this method of airframe shock testing in economic engineering, the prices of commodities are shocked, and the public consumer reaction is monitored. The resulting echoes of the economic shock are interpreted theoretically by computers and the psychic-economic structure of the economy is thus discovered. It is by this process that partial differential and difference matrices are discovered that define the family household and make possible its evaluation as an economic industry (dissipative consumer structure). Then the response of the household to future shocks can be predicted and manipulated, and society becomes a well-regulated animal with its reins under the control of a sophisticated computer-regulated social energy book-keeping system.

Eventually every individual element of the structure comes under control through a knowledge of personal preferences, such knowledge guaranteed by computer association of consumer preferences (universal product code-UPC-zebra stripe pricing codes on packages) with identified consumers (identified via association with the use of a credit card and later a permanent 'tattooed' body number invisible under normal ambient illumination.)

(K) Summary

Economics is only a social extension of a natural energy system. It also has its three passive components. Because of the distribution of wealth and the lack of communication and consequent lack of data, this field has been the last energy field for which a knowledge of these three passive components has been developed.

Since energy is the key to all activity on the face of the Earth, it follows that in order to attain a monopoly of energy, raw materials, goods, and services and to establish a world system of slave labor, it is necessary to have a first strike capability in the field of economics. In order to maintain our position, it is necessary that we have absolute first knowledge of the knowledge of the science of control over all economic factors and the first experience at engineering the world economy.

In order to achieve such sovereignty, we must at least achieve this one end: that the public will not make either the logical or mathematical connection between economics and the other energy sciences or learn to apply such knowledge.

This is becoming increasingly difficult to control because more and more businesses are making demands upon their computer programmers to create and apply mathematical models for the management of these businesses.

It is only a matter of time before the new breed of private programmer/economists will catch on to the far-reaching implications of the work begun at Harvard in 1948. The speed with which they can communicate their warning to the public will largely depend upon how effective we have been at controlling the media, subverting education and keeping the public distracted with matters of no real importance.

*Introduction to economic amplifiers:

Amplifiers are the active components of economic engineering. The basic characteristic of any amplifier (mechanical, electrical, or economic) is that it receives an input control signal and delivers energy from an independent energy source to a specified output terminal in a predictable relationship to that input control signal.

The simplest form of an economic amplifier is a device called advertising.

If a person is spoken to by a T.V. advertiser as if he were a twelve-year old, then, due to suggestibility, he will, with a certain probability, respond or react to that suggestion with the uncritical response of a twelve-year-old and will reach into his economic reservoir and deliver its energy to buy that product on impulse when he passes it in the store.

An economic amplifier may have several inputs and outputs. Its response might be instantaneous or delayed. Its circuit symbol might be a rotary switch if its options are exclusively qualitative, 'go' or 'no go', or it might have its parametric input/output relationships specified by a matrix with internal energy sources represented.

Whatever its form might be its purpose is to govern the flow of energy from a source to an output sink in direct relationship to an input control signal. For this reason, it is called an active circuit element or component.

In the design of an economic amplifier we must have some idea of at least five functions, which are:

1. The available input signals,
2. The desired output control objectives,

3. The strategic objective,

4. The available economic power sources,

5. The logistical options.

(L) Short List of inputs

*Questions to be answered: (1) what (2) when (3) where (4) how (5) why (6) who

*General sources of information: (1) telephone (2) surveillance (3) analysis of garbage (4) behavior in school

*Standard of living: (1) food (2) clothing (3) shelter (4) transportation *Social contacts: (1) telephone-itemized record of calls (2) family marriage certificates, etc. (3) friends, associates, etc. (4) memberships in organizations

*The personal paper trail: Personal buying habits, i.e...., personal consumer preferences: (1) checking accounts (2) credit card purchases (3) 'tagged' credit card purchase of products bearing U.P.C. (universal product code)

*Assets: (1) checking accounts (2) saving accounts (3) real estate (4) business (5) automobile (6) safety deposit at bank (7) stock market

*Liabilities: (1) creditors (2) enemies (see legal) (3) loans (4) consumer credit

*[so-called] Government sources (ploys): (1) welfare (2) social security

(3) U.S.D.A. (4) doles (5) grants (6) subsidies

* Government sources (via intimidation): (1) internal revenue service (2) OSHA (3) census (4) etc.

*Principal of this ploy-the citizen will almost always make the collection of information easy if he can operate on the 'free sandwich principle' of 'eat now and pay later.'

Other government sources-surveillance of U.S. mail

*Habit patterns-programming: strengths and weaknesses:

1. Activities (sports, hobbies, etc.)

2. See 'legal' (fear, anger, etc.-crime record)

3. Hospital records (drug sensitivities, reaction to pain, etc.)

4. Psychiatric records (fears, angers, disgusts, adaptability, reactions to stimuli, violence, suggestibility or hypnosis, pain, pleasure, love, and sex)

*Methods of coping:

1. Consumption of alcohol

2. Consumption of drugs

3. Entertainment

4. Religious factors influencing behavior

5. Other methods of escaping from reality

*Short list of outputs: outputs-create controlled situations. Manipulation of the economy, hence society. Control by controlling compensation and income.

Sequence:

1. Allocates opportunities

2. Destroys opportunities

3. Controls the economic environment

4. Controls the availability of raw materials

5. Controls capital

6. Controls bank rates

7. Controls the inflation of the currency

8. Controls the possession of property

9. Controls the industrial capacity

10. Controls manufacturing

11. Controls the availability of goods

12. Controls the prices of commodities
13. Controls services i.e. the labor force
14. Controls payments to so-called government officials
15. Controls the legal functions
16. Controls the personal data files-uncorrected by the party slandered
17. Controls advertising
18. Controls media content
19. Controls material available for T.V. viewing
20. Disengages attention from real issues
21. Engage emotions
22. Creates disorder, chaos, and insanity
23. Controls design of more probing tax forms
24. Controls surveillance
25. Controls the shortage of information
26. Develops psychological analyses and profiles of individuals
27. Controls sociological factors
28. controls health options
29. Prays on weaknesses
30. Cripples strengths
31. Leaches wealth and substance

*Table of Strategies:

Do	To, or To Get
(1) Keep public ignorant	(1) Less public organization
(2) access to control points [prices, sales]	(2) require reaction to outputs for feedback
(3) create preoccupation	(3) lower defenses
(4) attack the family unit	(4) control of the education of the young
(5) give them less cash and more credit and do less	(5) more self-indulgence and more data
(6) attack the privacy of the church	(6) destroy faith in this sort of government
(7) social conformity	(7) computer programming simplicity
(8) minimize tax protest	(8) maximum economic data/minimize enforcement problems
(9) stabilize consent coefficients	(9) simplicity
(10) tight control of variables	(10) simpler computer input data greater predictability
(11) establish boundary conditions	(11) problem simplicity/solution of differential and difference equations
(12) proper timing	(12) less data shift and blurring
(13) minimum resistance to control	(13) maximum control
(14) maximize control	(14) ultimate objective
(15) collapse of currency	(15) destroy the faith of the American people in each other

*Diversion: The primary strategy:

Experience has proven that the simplest method of securing a silent weapon and gaining control of the public is to keep the public undisciplined and ignorant of basic systems principles on the one hand while keeping them confused, disorganized, and distracted with matters of no real importance on the other hand.

This is achieved by:

1. Disengaging their minds, sabotaging their mental activities, by providing a low quality of program of public education in mathematics, logic, systems design, and economics; and by discouraging technical creativity.

2. Engaging their emotions, increasing their self-indulgence and their indulgence in emotional and physical activities by:

    - Unrelenting emotional affrontations and attacks (mental and emotional rape) by way of a constant barrage of sex, violence, and wars in the media-especially in the T.V. and the newspapers.

    - Giving them what they desire-in excess- 'junk food for thought'-and depriving them of what they really need.

3. Rewriting history and law and subjecting the public to the deviant creation; thus, being able to shift their thinking from personal needs to highly fabricated outside priorities.

These preclude their interest in, and discovery of, the silent weapons of social automation technology.

The general rule is that there is profit in confusion; the more confusion, the more profit. Therefore, the best approach is to create problems and then offer the solutions.

*Diversion summary:

- Media: keep the adult public attention diverted away from the real social issues and captivated by matters of no real importance.

- Schools: keep the young public ignorant of real mathematics, real economics, real law, and real history.

- Entertainment: keep the public entertainment below a sixth-grade level.
- Work: keep the public busy, busy, busy, with no time to think back on the farm with the other animals.

*Consent: The primary victory:

A silent weapon operates upon data obtained from a docile public by legal but not always lawful force. Much information is made available to silent weapon systems programmers, through the Internal Revenue Service. (see studies in the structure of the American economy for an I.R.S source list) this information consists of the enforced delivery of well-organized data obtained in federal and state tax forms collected, assembled, and submitted by slave labor, provided by taxpayers and employers. Furthermore, the number of such forms submitted to the I.R.S is a useful indicator for public consent, an important factor in strategic decision making. Other data sources are given in the short list of inputs.

*The artificial womb: from the time a person leaves its mother's womb, its every effort is directed toward building, maintaining, and withdrawing into artificial wombs, various sorts of substitute protective devices or shells.

The objective of these artificial wombs is to provide a stable environment for both stable and unstable activity; to provide a shelter for the evolutionary process of growth and maturity- i.e. survival; to provide security for freedom and to provide defensive protection from offensive activity.

This is equally true of both general public and the so-called elite. However, there is a difference in the way each of these "classes" go about the solution of problems.

The political structure of a nation: Dependency:

The primary reason why the individual citizens of a country create a political structure is a subconscious wish or desire to perpetuate their own dependency relationship of childhood. So, they hire politicians to face reality for them.

*Summary: People hire politicians so that the people can:

1. Obtain security without managing it.
2. Obtain action without thinking about it.

3. Inflict theft, injury, and death upon others without having to contemplate either life and death.

4. Avoid responsibility for their own intentions.

5. Obtain the benefits of reality and science without exerting themselves in the discipline of facing or learning either of these things.

Chapter 5: Outwitting the Devil

(A) Self-Defense

1. Do your own thinking on all occasions. The fact that human beings are given complete control over nothing save the power to think their own thoughts is laden with significance.

2. Decide definitely what you want from life; then create a plan for attaining it and be willing to sacrifice everything else, if necessary, rather than accept permanent defeat.

3. Analyze temporary defeat, no matter of what nature or cause, and extract from it the seed of an equivalent advantage.

4. Be willing to render useful service equivalent to the value of all material things you demand of life and render the service first.

5. Recognize that your brain is a receiving set that can be attuned to receive communications from the universal storehouse of infinite knowledge, to help you transmute your desires into their physical equivalent.

6. Recognize that your greatest asset is time, the only thing except the power of thought which you own outright, and the one thing which can be shaped into whatever material things you want. Budget your time so none of it is wasted.

7. Recognize the truth that fear generally is a filler with which the "devil" occupies the unused portion of your mind. It is only a state of mind which you can control by filling the space it occupies with faith in your ability to make life provide you with whatever you demand of it.

8. When you pray, do not beg! Demand what you want and insist upon getting exactly that, with no substitutes.

9. Recognize that life is a cruel taskmaster and that either you master it, or it masters you. There is no half-way or compromising point. Never accept from life anything you do not want. If that which you do not want is temporarily forced upon you, you can refuse, in your own mind, to accept it and it will make way for the thing you do want.

10. Lastly, remember that your dominating thoughts attract, through a definite law of nature, by the shortest and most convenient route, their physical counterpart. Be careful what your thoughts dwell upon.

(B) Education

- Reverse the present system by giving children the privilege of leading in their school work instead of following orthodox rules designed only to impart abstract knowledge. Let instructors serve as students and let the students serve as instructors.

- As far as possible, organize all school work into definite methods through which the student can learn by doing, and direct the class work so that every student engages in some form of practical labor connected with the daily problems of life.

- Ideas are the beginning of all human achievement. Teach all students how to recognize practical ideas that may be of benefit in helping them acquire whatever they demand of life.

- Teach the students how to budget and use time, and above all teach the truth that time is the greatest asset available to human beings and the cheapest.

- Teach the student the basic motives by which all people are influenced and show how to use these motives in acquiring the necessities and the luxuries of life.

- Teach children what to eat, and what is the relationship between proper eating and sound health.

- Teach children the true nature and function of the emotion of sex, and above all, teach them that it can be transmitted into a driving force capable of lifting one to great heights of achievement.

- Teach children to be definite in all things, beginning with the choice of a definite major purpose in life!

- Teach children the nature of and possibilities for good and evil in the principle of habit, using as illustration with which to dramatize the subject of everyday experiences of children and adults.

- Teach children how habits become fixed through the law of hypnotic rhythm, and influence them to adopt, while in the lower grades, habits that will lead to independent thought!

- Teach children the difference between temporary defeat and failure and show them how to search for the seed of an equivalent advantage which comes with every defeat.

- Teach children to express their own thoughts fearlessly and to accept or reject, at will, all ideas of others, reserving to themselves, always, the privilege of relying upon their own judgment.

- Teach children to reach decisions promptly and to change them, if at all, slowly and with reluctance, and never without a definite reason.

- Teach children that the human brain is the instrument with which one receives, from the great storehouse of nature, the energy which is specialized into definite thoughts; that the brain does not think but serves as an instrument for the interpretation of stimuli which cause thought.

- Teach children the value of harmony in their own minds and that this is attainable only through self-control.

- Teach children the nature and value of self-control.

- Teach children that there is a law of increasing returns which can be and should be put into operations, as a matter of habit, by rendering always more service and better service than is expected of them.

- Teach children the true nature of the golden rule, and above all show them that through creation of this principle, everything they do to and for another they do for themselves.

- Teach children not to have opinions unless they are formed from facts or beliefs which may reasonably be accepted as facts.

- Teach children that cigarettes, liquor, narcotics, and over indulgence in sex destroys the power of will and lead to the habit of drifting. Do not forbid these evils-just explain them.

- Teach children the danger of believing anything merely because their parents, religious instructors, or someone else says it is so.

- Teach children to face facts, whether they are pleasant or unpleasant, without resorting to subterfuge or offering alibis.

- Teach children to encourage the use of their sixth-sense through which ideas present themselves in their minds from unknown sources, and to examine all such ideas carefully.

- Teach children the full import of the law of compensation and show them how the law works in the small, everyday affairs of life.

- Teach children that definiteness of purpose, backed by definite plans persistently and continuously applied, is the most efficacious form of prayer available to human beings.

- Teach children that the space they occupy in the world is measured definitely by the quality and quantity of useful service they render in the world.

- Teach children there is no problem which does not have an appropriate solution and that the solution often may be found in the circumstance creating the problem.

- Teach children that their only real limitations are those which they set up or permit others to establish in their own minds.

- Teach them that man can achieve whatever man can conceive and believe!

- Teach children that all schoolhouses and all textbooks are elementary implements which may be helpful in the development of their minds, but that the only school of real value is the great university of life wherein one has the privilege of learning from experience.

- Teach children to be true to themselves at all times and, since they cannot please everybody, therefore to do a good job of pleasing themselves.

(C) Disharmony/Self-sabotage

- Overeating-leads to ill health and misery.

- Over-indulgence in sex-breaks down one's will power and leads to the habit of drifting.

- Negative thoughts-envy, greed, fear, hatred, intolerance, vanity, self-pity, or discouragement, these states of mind lead to the habit of drifting.

- Guile-cheating, lies, and stealing destroy self-respect, subdue one's conscience, and lead to unhappiness.

- Ignorance-leads to poverty and loss of self-reliance.
- Non-discriminant-accepting from life anything one does not want indicates an unpardonable neglect to use the mind.
- Drifting-leads to poverty and destroys the privilege of self-determination. It also deprives one of the privilege of using his own mind as a medium of contact with infinite intelligence.

(D) Spiritual bribes/traps:

- Love
- The thirst for sexual expression
- Covetousness for money
- The obsessive desire to gain something for nothing-gambling
- Vanity in women, egotism in men
- Desire to be the master of others
- Desire for intoxicants and narcotics
- Desire for self-expression through words and deeds
- Desire to imitate others
- Desire for perpetuation of life after death
- Desire to be a hero or heroine
- Desire for physical food

(E) 6 fears of man

1. Poverty
2. Criticism
3. Ill health
4. Loss of love
5. Old age

6. Death

(F) Controlled Sex

- Supplies the magnetic force that attracts people to one another. It is the most important factor of a pleasing personality.

- It gives quality to the tone of voice and enables one to convey through the voice any feeling desired.

- It serves, as nothing else can serve, to give motive-power to one's desires.

- It keeps the nervous system charged with energy needed to carry on the work of maintaining the body.

- It sharpens the imagination and enables one to create useful ideas.

- It gives quickness and definiteness to one's physical and mental movements.

- It gives one persistence and perseverance in the pursuit of one's major purpose in life.

- It is a great antidote for all fear.

- It gives one immunity against discouragement.

- It helps to master laziness and procrastination.

- It gives one physical and mental endurance while undergoing any form of opposition.

- It gives one the fighting qualities necessary under all circumstances for self-defense.

(G) Fear and Faith

"Fear is the tool of a man-made devil. Self-confident faith in one's self is both the man-made weapon which defeats this devil and the man-made tool which builds a triumphant life. And it is more than that. It is a link to the irresistible forces of the universe which stand behind a man who does not believe in failure and defeat as being anything but temporary experiences."- Napoleon Hill

What is faith? It is a state of mind wherein one recognizes and uses the power of positive thought as a medium by which one contacts and draws upon the universal store of infinite intelligence at will. The absence of all forms of negative thought.

(H) 9 gates of hell

- Fear
- Superstition
- Avarice
- Greed
- Lust
- Revenge
- Anger
- Vanity
- laziness

(I) 7 principles of freedom (Heaven)

1. Definiteness of purpose
2. Mastery over self
3. Learning from adversity
4. Controlling environmental influence (associations)
5. Time (giving permanency to positive, rather than negative thought-habits and developing wisdom)
6. Harmony (acting with definiteness of purpose to become the dominating influence in your own mental, spiritual, and physical environment)
7. Caution (thinking through your plans before you act)

(J) Self-Diagnosis

hey, listen to your emotions...

Bitterness shows you where you need to heal, where you're still holding judgments on others and yourself.

Resentment shows you where you're living in the past and not allowing the present to be as it is.

Discomfort shows you that you need to pay attention right now to what is happening, because you're being given the opportunity to change, to do something different than you typically do it.

Anger shows you what you're passionate about, where your boundaries are, and what you believe needs to change about the world.

Disappointment shows you that you tried for something, that you did not give in to apathy, that you still care.

Guilt shows you that you're still living life in other people's expectations of what you should do.

Shame shows you that you're internalizing other people's beliefs about who you should be (or who you are) and that you need to reconnect with yourself.

Anxiety shows you that you need to wake up, right now, and that you need to be present, that you're stuck in the past and living in fear of the future.

Sadness shows you the depth of your feeling, the depth of your care for others and this world.

23 EMOTIONS PEOPLE FEEL, BUT CAN'T EXPLAIN

1. **Sonder**: The realization that each passerby has a life as vivid and complex as your own.
2. **Opia**: The ambiguous intensity of looking someone in the eye, which can feel simultaneously invasive and vulnerable.
3. **Monachopsis**: The subtle but persistent feeling of being out of place.
4. **Énouement**: The bittersweetness of having arrived in the future, seeing how things turn out, but not being able to tell your past self.
5. **Vellichor**: The strange wistfulness of used bookshops.
6. **Rubatosis**: The unsettling awareness of your own heartbeat.
7. **Kenopsia**: The eerie, forlorn atmosphere of a place that is usually bustling with people but is now abandoned and quiet.
8. **Mauerbauertraurigkeit**: The inexplicable urge to push people away, even close friends who you really like.
9. **Jouska**: A hypothetical conversation that you compulsively play out in your head.
10. **Chrysalism**: The amniotic tranquility of being indoors during a thunderstorm.
11. **Vemödalen**: The frustration of photographic something amazing when thousands of identical photos already exist.
12. **Anecdoche**: A conversation in which everyone is talking, but nobody is listening.
13. **Ellipsism**: A sadness that you'll never be able to know how history will turn out.
14. **Kuebiko**: A state of exhaustion inspired by acts of senseless violence.
15. **Lachesism**: The desire to be struck by disaster – to survive a plane crash, or to lose everything in a fire.
16. **Exulansis**: The tendency to give up trying to talk about an experience because people are unable to relate to it.
17. **Adronitis**: Frustration with how long it takes to get to know someone.
18. **Rückkehrunruhe**: The feeling of returning home after an immersive trip only to find it fading rapidly from your awareness.
19. **Nodus Tollens**: The realization that the plot of your life doesn't make sense to you anymore.
20. **Onism**: The frustration of being stuck in just one body, that inhabits only one place at a time.
21. **Liberosis**: The desire to care less about things.
22. **Altschmerz**: Weariness with the same old issues that you've always had – the same boring flaws and anxieties that you've been gnawing on for years.
23. **Occhiolism**: The awareness of the smallness of your perspective.

Chapter 6: 11 Lessons on Leadership

(A) Curiosity

1. Good questions are more important than easy answers. The "silly question" is often not silly at all, it's the beginning of a new pathway toward a solution. "The most important thing is not to stop the questioning."-Albert Einstein. All great ideas, works of art, are based on curiosity.

2. Curiosity is a process. It is fundamentally about creating a driving force in your life, innerstanding that force and always challenging it through self-evaluation and questioning. In other words, one of the most important characteristics one must possess for success in a word that is predicated on the survival of the fittest is an interest in life, good, bad, or peculiar.

3. Curiosity should always be challenging and always solidify a sense of commitment. The objective is to solve the problem, to win the game, to get past the place where you might have been stuck. The dream of winning slips away with the loss of curiosity. Though curiosity is a child's possession, an adult can use it consciously as a tool, can cultivate it in the building of a winning strategy. It does not matter if the game is running a fortune 500 company or a family, curiosity leads to innerstanding/overstanding (your competition, your colleagues, your loved ones) and ultimately to the implementation of plans. Curiosity should be a verb, not a noun. Curiosity is connected to doing, solving, experimenting, trying, failing, and then accomplishing. "How does this work?" "What do I do?" "What happens next?" "What do I do to make this turn out the way I want-or the way you want?" "How do I get from here to there?" "What can I do to help you (or myself)?" Those are all basic questions that stem from curiosity, but that are also basic to wining.

(B) Ego

1. Establish your business culture around your team. A business culture in its simplest form is nothing more than the environment in which decisions are made. All business cultures, all units, succeed or fail on the basis of the decision they make. So, the concept of team

ego is a factor in getting people to see success not in terms of individual performance but rather in getting more fulfillment from the group's success.

2. Vest people in the process. Help everyone on the team understand/innerstand where the group is going, how it is going to get there, and, most important, why sharing decision making is a critical step in achieving ego.

3. Create unselfishness as the most important team characteristic.

(C) Listening

1. Listening is more important than talking. When you are an active listener, you are respecting what the other being is feeling or expressing.

2. Listening is a skill that requires you to subordinate your own views when listening to someone else. The more you practice the more you will be able to distinguish, for yourself, the difference between hearing and listening. Start by keeping the mouth tightly closed. To become an effective listener, you may have to break some bad habits.

3. Convert our listening skills to effective language skills. Once you have learned to listen, become especially mindful of the kinds of words and phrases you use that will help others listen to you more effectively. Listening is ultimately about effective communication, and everyone can benefit from that. The effort and practice of effective listening has a big payoff in every facet of life. It is a basic but powerful human need to be understood, and the effective listener is filling that need as well as gaining information that he or she may need.

*6 bad habits of listening:

- Do you find yourself trying to come up with a "better" story than the one the speaker is telling?

- Are you nodding yes when you are not really listening just to keep the conversation moving?

- Do you make eye contact with the speaker?

- Do you find you forget what has been said immediately following the conversation?

- Are you asking trivial questions to seem as if you are listening?

- Are you always interrupting because you feel you have a "more important" thing to say?

(D) Toughness or tenderness: creating your leadership style

1. Successful teams of any kind are benevolent dictatorships. If you lead wisely, you'll be followed cheerfully.

2. Be adaptable. Great leaders can follow as well as lead. It's the difference between an outside-in leader and an inside-out leader.

   Outside-in leaders are always finding ways to include others, to use, draw out, and promote others in their counsels and decision-making. Inside-out leaders rely solely on their own intuition, logic, and counsel, which they then project outward in the form of commands.

3. Real kindness is an act of strength and a tremendous leadership asset.

   *Remember the 5 most important words:

   "I am proud of you."

   *Remember the 4 most important words:

   "What is your opinion?"

   *Remember the 3 most important words:

   "I appreciate that."

   *Remember the 2 most important words:

   "Thank you."

   *Remember the most important word

   "You (I)."

(E) Invisibility

1. Invisibility is an extra dimension, an "X-factor" that can be used, if innerstood, in relationships on all levels; personal, corporate, and collective. It allows the "invisible"

being or entity the chance to augment its power, to appear unexpectedly, to have the knowledge no one anticipated, to intimidate rather than to muscle the competition.

2. Invisibility can be used as a practical tool, but only at the point when we recognize that others may not see us as we are (or may not see us at all). When that is innerstood, when we make the conscious effort to see that we are not seen, we can then put ourselves into position to define ourselves on our terms. The ability to do this is fundamental in any successful relationship whether it is in business or at home.

3. Invisibility opens doors, creates opportunity where none seemed to exist before. When we ae unseen, we have an enormous advantage in moving in, in doing things we wish or need to do, and in the process to change the very dynamic of existing, seemingly closed, patterns.

(F) Craftsmanship

1. Learning is a daily experience and a lifetime mission. Innerstand why you are succeeding and build on it.

2. Craftsmanship and quality are never an accident. Craftsmanship is the result of sincere effort, principled intentions, intelligent direction, and skillful execution. Craftsmanship is the highest choice of many alternatives.

3. Make craftsmanship contagious. Players on great teams learn from each other. The lifetime of experiences we bring to each relationship is a gift to be shared. An entire team working to be the best will be the best.

(G) Personal integrity

1. Take responsibility for everything you do. The first day of practice is the beginning of a championship season. The first memo in the mourning is the beginning of the introduction of a new idea.

2. Stand behind the choices you make. No leader can manage with

    "buts". That means committing yourself to under/inner/overstanding what goes into a choice: the information you have at your disposal, the competing arguments, everything that you will need to provide you with a willingness rather than an excuse to make a choice.

3. Be fully present in whatever you are doing. That means giving all of yourself to a task at hand. That sounds easy enough, but it isn't, because there are so many ways to back off, to move away, to let others do for you what you know you have to do for yourself and your team.

(H) Rebounding

1. Rebounding is both the end of the defense and the beginning of the offense. It is always an affirmative act and never a reaction. That you are able to rebound should always mean you ae ready to take control of the situation.

2. Give up the victim mentality.

3. Resilience is essential. Resiliency, like rebounding, involves balance. One cannot win without resilience.

(I) Imagination

1. Imagination is a way of applying innovation and seeing a positive rather than a negative. It's better to light a candle than curse the darkness.

2. An idea can be a feat of association. Good ideas are more often the stringing together of experiences, observations, and thoughts in a way that no one has done before. Good ideas make great conclusions.

3. Visualization is a practical skill that can be sharpened through exercise. Seeing yourself and others in your "game" brings not only familiarity, but also the ability to see past the obvious to the nuance that can be the difference between winning and not winning. Visualization puts your imagination to work. I have found that this still is critical to winning.

(J) Discipline, delegation, and decision-making

1. All choices must be made with a clear and attainable objective in mind, even if it is only to move the process from point A to point B in an alphabet of points before success is assured. Decisions made without clear plans in mind ae likely to create confusion, resentment, and failure. Others will quickly recognize it when plans are not spelled out, and even if there is a residue of good feeling for the decision maker, a subtle sense of uneasiness and uncertainty will tend to be undermining.

2. Delegating authority in decision-making can only take place successfully when there is absolute confidence in those to whom power is given. In delegating, the process is always about teamwork, not about surrendering responsibility. The objective in delegating is to make the team better, whether it is a corporation, a university, or a unit. In delegating you must do everything possible to remain in active touch with those to whom power of communication has been given. Make delegating a process of communication rather than the giving up of anything.

3. Think everything through first, then stick your neck out. Making no decision is far more dangerous than making the wrong decision.

(K) Everyone can win

1. Look for an opportunity to win in any situation. Don't wait for a promotion or a better job. Ask yourself, always, what does it take to win today? Don't overlook it.

2. You have to be the one to determine how to measure winning. That means making sure you do not allow others to define how the game is going to be played. You have to familiarize yourself with the standards of your work. If expertise is what it takes, you have to do whatever is necessary to make yourself an expert, but it is always up to you to make sure you innerstand the crucial difference between doing something well or poorly. That's the real difference between winning and losing. If you are true with yourself, you will be true with everyone else, you will win no matter where you are, no matter what you are doing.

3. Start now, not tomorrow. This is essential because it means that you commit yourself wherever you find yourself.

Chapter 7: THE 24 DOMINANT LAWS OF THE SUBCONSCIOUS MIND by Lloyd Dison

First Law: All hypnosis is self-hypnosis and is any altered state of mind or focus. It is a dreamlike imaginary state between the awake state and the sleep state. Your eyes can be open or closed in each of the states of hypnosis. A hypnotist guides you into a dreamlike state, where the subconscious mind takes each suggestion as a reality.

Second Law: Everyone goes in and out of hypnosis 100 to 200 times per day. It is said that each of us goes into the deep dream or REM (Rapid Eye Movement) state from 7 to 8 times per day on our own.

Third Law: The subconscious mind represents about 90% of your mind power, the conscious mind, about 10%.

Fourth Law: You are not your body. You are a perfect spirit child of God living within this physical body.

Fifth Law: You are but a memory. 100% of everything you have ever thought, dreamed and experienced is stored in your bodies and minds as memories.

Sixth Law: The subconscious mind is fully developed at birth to: (1) keep you alive — flight or fight, fear of loud noises, fear of falling; (2) keep you happy — to get attention, recognition or approval (positive or negative). These laws reverse immediately after birth. Keeping you happy, in its interpretation, is dominant and becomes more important than keeping you alive. Its interpretation of "happy" means happy or miserable.

Seventh Law: Events and trials are stored in your bodies as living chemical memories at the moment they occurred. Each event is alive and well and ready to manifest in you physically, mentally, emotionally, and spiritually, from anything which can trigger these stored events. The subconscious mind can access all memories in the physical body as if they were its own.

Eighth Law: Your major problems were programmed into your memories in your first twelve years, like a series of dominoes. Any problems and trials after age twelve are simply triggers or symptoms of the first events.

Ninth Law: All dominant thoughts become programs or habits. All habits are from the subconscious mind, including everything you think, say and do automatically from habit.

Tenth Law: It takes 21 days to six weeks to consciously create a new habit or program. The subconscious can accept a new habit program instantly.

Eleventh Law: When you fight a habit, it will always win. Think about a pink elephant with green and black toenails. Then try to not think about a pink elephant with green and black toenails.

Twelfth Law: All habits can become addictions. The level of addictions is equal to the level of low self-esteem in your first twelve years.

Thirteenth Law: The subconscious mind knows no difference between reality and imagination. Only your conscious mind can see, hear, smell, taste and touch — your five senses. The subconscious mind can only use imagination for programming and response. Use your imagination and think about biting into a lemon or dill pickle, then notice the twinge in your jaw and perhaps saliva in your mouth.

Fourteenth Law: The subconscious mind is programmed like a computer. You program your subconscious mind positively or negatively through self-hypnosis by 1) visualization (clear picture), 2) affirmation, and 3) activation by dynamic emotions or experiences.

Fifteenth Law: What you see is what you get, or What you focus on, you create or recreate. (Even if what you see is only in your imagination or mind.)

Sixteenth Law: You create your tomorrows today (this moment — this second) by what you see, hear, smell, taste, feel, think, say, do, and experience.

Seventeenth Law: Your subconscious mind is like a robot and must, and always does, deliver your dominant thoughts, from birth to death (positive or negative). Dominant subconscious programs manifest in your conscious awake state physically, mentally, emotionally and spiritually.

Eighteenth Law: Your subconscious mind always misinterprets, confuses or reverses a message unless your conscious mind or another person helps you translate it correctly. The program for addictions is set by eighteen months of age.

Nineteenth Law: In order to obtain a new modality or reality in your life, you must decide what you do want, let go (forgive your past) and then activate your faith and accept your future as a reality, now in the present.

Twentieth Law: Will power is weak and is strengthened by writing down your desires and affirmations. Will power can then help your conscious mind program and control the subconscious mind.

Twenty-First Law: You must change your thoughts and language in order to keep a new program, or you will rehypnotize yourself back into the same old program you had before.

Twenty-Second Law: You manifest a positive desire by acceptance of the desire as a reality — release and act "as-if."

Twenty-Third Law: The Subconscious mind is just a program and was designed to give you trials. The glory and kingdom of the next life will be determined by the way you handle your trials in this life.

Twenty-Fourth Law: Your subconscious mind works all night on the last thought you have before sleep. Be sure of what you pray for and visualize before going to sleep.

*4 Essential health warnings:

- Don't abuse your heart by allowing your brain to physically harm it by exposing it to constant stress and straining toward self-fulfillment.
- Don't exploit your heart by allowing your brain to misappropriate its miraculous energy for selfish purposes.
- Don't deprive your heart by allowing your brain's innate selfishness to distance you from the hearts of others.
- Don't neglect your heart by allowing your brain to be so busily and reactively consumed with trying to stay alive that it forgets to allow time for your heart to proactively reflect on what purposes you chose for your living.

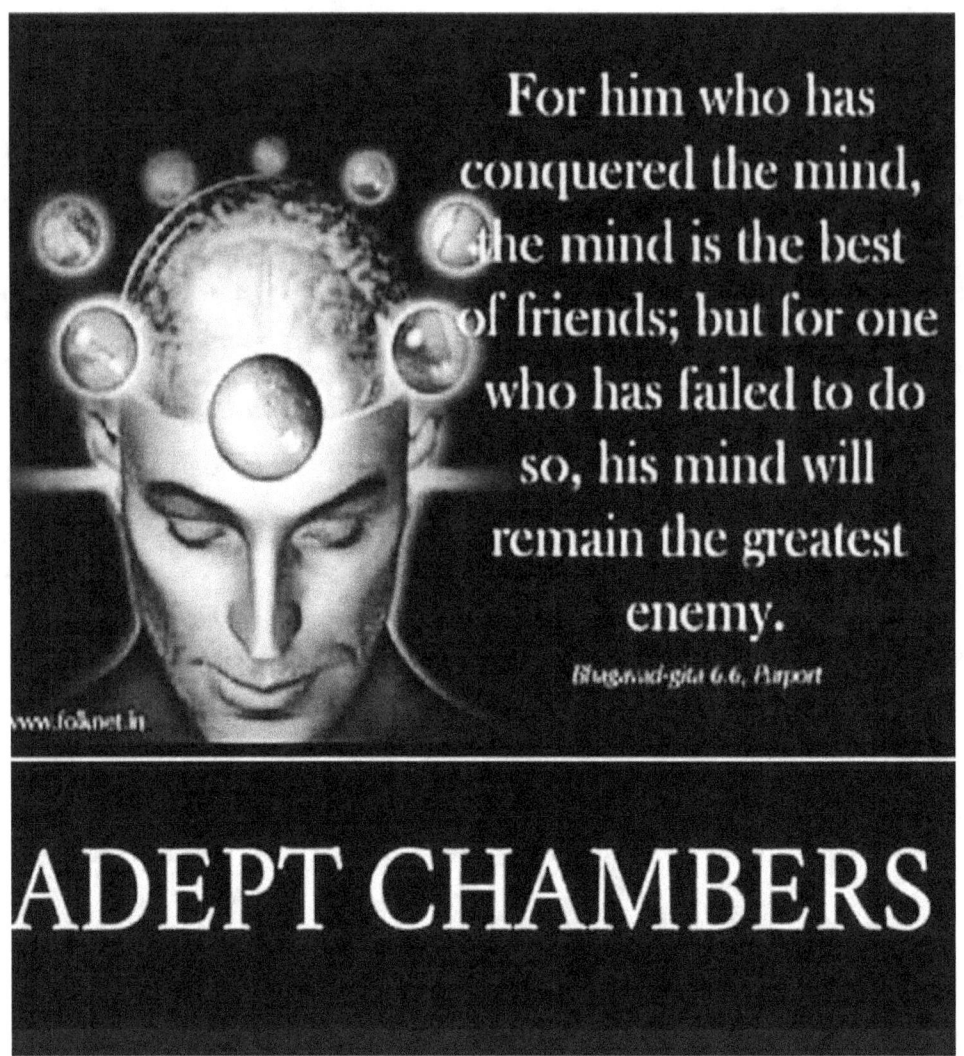

"True teaching is not an accumulation of knowledge; it is an awakening of consciousness that goes through successive stages."
- Ancient Egyptian Proverb

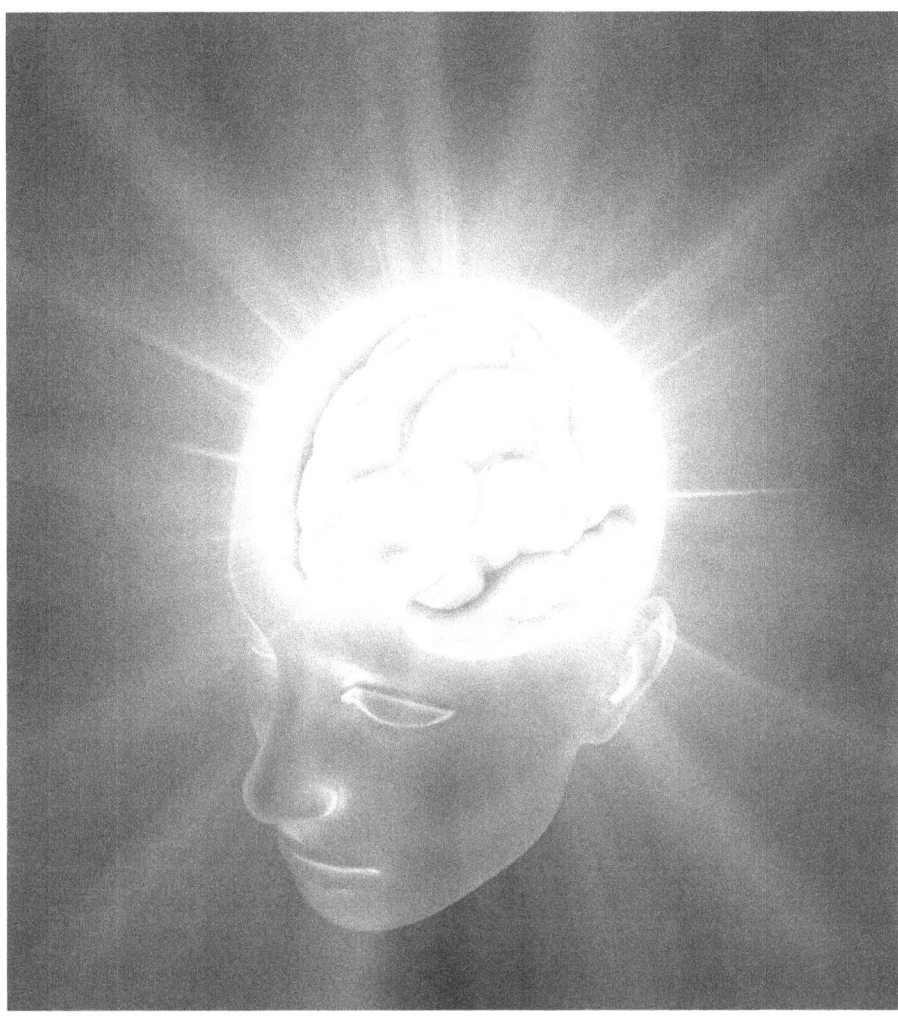

"No problem can be solved by the same level of consciousness that created it."
- Albert Einstein

Romans 12:2- Do not conform to this world but <u>be ye transformed by the renewing of your mind</u>. Then you will be able to test and approve what God's will is-his good, pleasing and perfect will.

Part 3: G.O.D.-Generator, Operator, Destroyer

What! Know ye not that your body is the temple of the Holy Ghost which is in you, which ye have of God, and ye are not your own? -I Corinthians 6:19

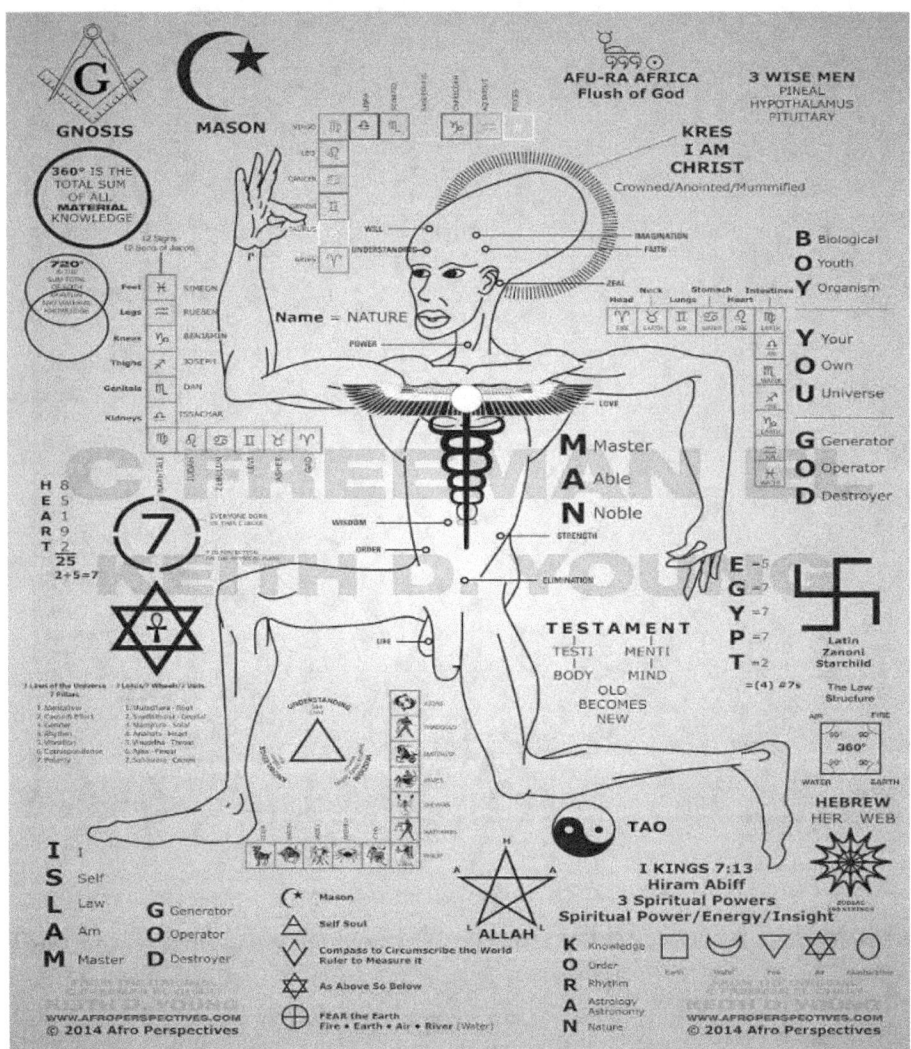

1 Corinthians 3:16 Know ye not that ye are the temple of God, and that the Spirit of God dwelleth in you?

Chapter 1: Stages of Spiritual Growth

1. Reliance on the part of being with limited knowledge and capability; polarization in learning from outside ourselves (someone else); reliance on externals (tools, machinery, medicines, etc.)

2. Reliance on the part of being with infinite knowledge and capability; in learning from within ourselves; polarization in reliance on internals (the power of spirit.)

3. The equilibrium between the two, utilizing both internal and external approaches to existence.

*True religion deals with the techniques of communicating with the director of the automation within us, in order to gain access to the power, storehouse of information, and the host of shaping factors of our lives.

*Brief Definition of Religion:

Moorish Latin prefix "re" meaning "again, back" + "ligare" meaning "tie, bind, fasten", as well as the Indo-European root "leg" meaning "to collect" from whence the Greek "legein" and Moorish Latin "legere" meaning "logic" and "legal". From this we can conclude that the ancient founders and coiners of religion applied it to those beliefs and practices aimed at tying people back to something with which they had originally been one and belong with natural connectivity i.e. the mind (common sense; reasoning; balance). The original oneness is implied by the prefix "re" (back, again), and the natural connectivity is explicit in the root meaning "law and logic". Right at the outset we can see that in the meaning of the word itself, according to its components, religion was not thought to be opposed to reason, logic and law, which are the foundations of science, and philosophy but united.

Chapter 2: The manifestation of God in Man

The Creator's Essential Attributes	Manifesting in Man's daily life
(1) Omnipresence	In the early stages of man's growth, it manifests itself as the sense of humanity, and oneness between men, and between man and his environment. The urge to seek and establish peace and cooperation. In the latter part of man's growth, it manifests in us as the ability to experience all other men and things in the world as a part of our being, as we now experience the separate parts of our bodies as belonging to the whole.
(2) Omniscience	In the early stages of man's growth, it manifests as the capacity to solve, over time all problems in life. All discoveries and knowledge in the world were intuited by someone. In the latter part of life, it manifests as the ability to go into trance and discover the solution to any problem, on demand.
(3) Omnipotence	The manifestation of psychic powers which have made themselves known through a number of beings throughout history. While in the west, these appear at random, they are deliberately and methodically cultivated-i.e., scientifically-by Orientals.

For in him dwelleth all the fullness of the Godhead bodily. And **Ye are complete** in him, which **is the head** of all principality and power. - Colossians 2:9-10

Chapter 3: Spiritual Eyes

For we wrestle not against flesh and blood, but against principalities, against powers, against rulers of the darkness of this world, against spiritual wickedness, in high places. Ephesians 6:12

Many people are facing spiritual struggles as they attempt to advance in the things of the Most High God, within. One of the primary tricks of the enemy is to get a person deceived and not realizing the depth of what is taking place in their lives and the lessons to be learned.

Oftentimes people assume that the struggle they are facing is just a natural battle yet just beneath the surface there is something far more complex taking place. They are under a spiritual attack where their chakras are being blocked and their thoughts manipulated!

What Is A Spiritual Attack? A spiritual attack is a series of events coordinated by the demonic realm also known as the lower nature. Negative thoughts can come from self, or negative thoughts can come from others. These events set into motion generated from others through something as simple as bad mouthing or thinking badly about oneself.

The auric field can be strengthened so that the lower thought forms bounces off and has no effect on the intended. Auric strengthening techniques are chanting, negative thought rearrangement, prayer, affirmation, meditation, and/or chi gung exercises. There is so many ways to cleans the auric field from Spiritual Attack.

Many people wrongly assume their thoughts have no effects on their everyday experiences, yet these same thoughts are utilized to do things throughout the day. After all thoughts, actions, and behavior go hand in hand since the beginning of time.

Negative karma is created by negative interactions with people! We must not be ignorant to the strategies of the enemy. We can no longer live our lives with our spiritual eyes undeveloped. We must also walk in the spirit and be aware of what is taking place around us physically and spiritually. How can you identify a spiritual attack? Here are 8 symptoms of an attack and solutions to apply:

1. **Lack of spiritual passion:** to feel weakness or to procrastinate on a regular basis. To act as if you have no spiritual work or have slack or stalled on any practices. Your commitments or words are tested, and it doesn't align with truth. Having issue with following through. Meditation is great for enhancing spiritual passion. Candle magic also gives a physical counterpart to the spiritual. These techniques get stronger and stronger as one practices them daily.

2. **Extreme frustration:** during a spiritual attack the enemy uses a variety of circumstances to oppress the mind and bring great frustration. A being who is under siege finds themselves on edge and anxious. Unable to think their way to a solution. Short-tempered and mean to those that are on their team or in their unit. Deep breathing is a fantastic way to eliminate frustration and to bring clarity. Rubbing the $1^{st}/3^{rd}$ eye area between the brow is also a good way to rid the mind of frustration.

3. **Confusion about purpose:** during a spiritual attack there is often great confusion about spiritual direction. This is one of the chief goals of an attack, to get a being out of their destiny. Everyone has a destiny that is unveiled in their solar return day. the 2nd house of one's birth chart unveils what works one should be doing. When you have a blue print, frustrations are minimized, and your purpose is recognized once revealed.

4. **Lack of peace:** negative attacks make uneasy the mind with various thoughts and ongoing temptation in order to rob you of peace. The mind becomes irritated and exhausted. Mental fatigue is a stagnation to peace. Wearing all white or fasting resonate with peace. Not eating or smoking allows the body to rest and catch up with stored work.

5. **Unusually sluggish and tired:** A lack of energy and vitality are often the result of an extended attack. Garbing oneself with golden lights as if you are standing in front of the sun gives lots of energy to melaninated cells. Is a perfect way to rejuvenate the body. While in this mind state send back the negative energy with a cant created off the dome. These are very effective and grow stronger every time they are used.

6. **Strong urge to quit assignment:** Every Natural being is born with a purpose. These purposes are found within the truth of your north and south nodes. When a person is living in their purpose doors open in various areas: They will receive everything that's

needed to fulfill their purpose and life's destiny. It's important to vibrate satisfaction and fulfillment while living out your destiny this will reward you and bring abundance. Simply put, haters step up their negative thoughts towards you when they see you resonating on and towards your purpose. This unfortunately is an indication that you need to keep your ideas to yourself. During an attack you'd feel overwhelmed with thoughts and desires to give up! This is one of his greatest purposes behind spiritual attacks to keep you stagnated.

7. **Drawn back towards old bondages:** In a long spiritual battle a person is often pulled back towards negative cycles that they broke free from. The hater feels better to see you back into the same old bondages. If your hater can discourage you bad enough to give into stagnation than they feel more comfortable with not fulfilling their life's mission. Solutions for this is to have a goal sheet. Write out everything you'd like to happen in your life and give a time frame for when it should be occurring to add more power to your manifestations.

8. Questioning direction and call that was one so clear: As a hater attacks the life of a God/Goddess you can tell because you begin to give reasons to give up on your life's mission instead of solutions on how to get there. You'll know because confusion, shame, intimidation and a variety of vile schemes to create a cloud of uncertainty.
You'll deeply questioning the road that they you're traveling. Usually they begin to reexamine decisions that were once crystal clear.
Oftentimes a person in the midst of an attack will question words of wisdom, spiritual breakthroughs, dreams, mediations, signs, symbols, and significant experiences that they had. This is a step towards moving backwards in your spiritual growth. A solution for this is to cleanse with sliced fresh lemons in your bath water. This is a powerful practice. A fresh whole lemon can also be carried in your pocket or purse as well, until it turns dark then add it to the compost or bury it in the yard. Crystals that will assist in addition to the lemon are calligraphy stone, amethyst, laborite, and/or nuumite.

3 additional Steps To not be harmed by Spiritual attack:

1. Break it with your words: You've got to know inside yourself the power you possess that can break spiritual attack.

2. Break it with prayer/meditation: Affirm a prayer that rhymes or a song that encourages you. Get into a schedule where you will meditate often around the same time. Go to a peaceful place in nature or near water.

3. Break it with discipline: Challenge yourself to submit to your higher self. The God force that lies within will not lead you incorrectly. However, the key is to strengthen the voice and the ability to recognize this force that lies within when it moves you. An energy that's closer than your jugular.

Chapter 4: The Force of 12

(A) 12 powers of man (galactic)

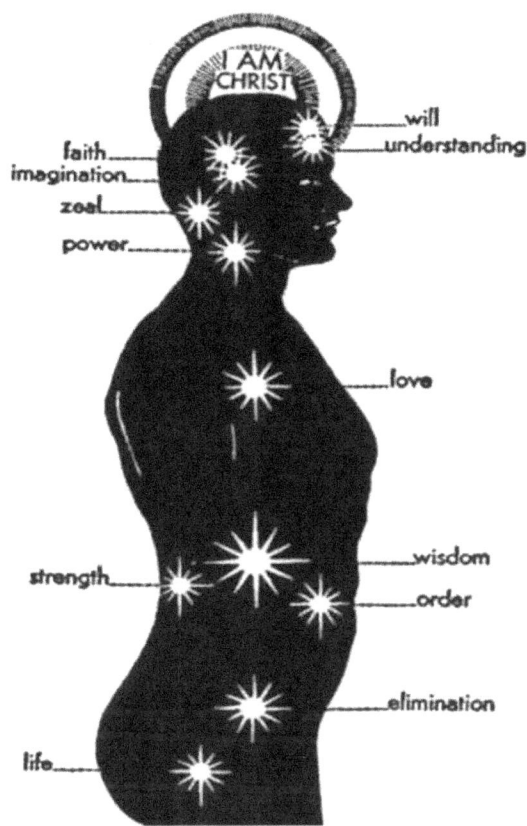

The subconscious realm in man has 12 great centers of action, with 12 residing egos of identities. When Yeshua had attained a certain soul development, he called his 12 apostles to him. This means that when man is cultivating out of mere personal consciousness into spiritual consciousness, he begins to train deeper and larger powers; he sends his thought down into the inner centers of his organism, and through his word quickens them to life. Where before his powers have worked in the personal, now they begin to expand and work in the universal. This is the first and the second coming of Krist, spoken of in the scriptures. The first coming is the receiving of truth into the conscious mind, and the second coming is the awakening and the regeneration of the subconscious of Kerest mind (collective/galactic).

Man expands and grows under divine evolution as an industrial plant grows. As the business expands, it is found that system is necessary. Instead of one man's being able to do the work with the assistance of a few helpers, he requires many helpers. Instead of a few helpers, he needs hundreds; and in order to promote efficiency he must have heads for the various departments of the work. Scripture symbology calls the heads of departments in man's consciousness the twelve apostles.

Each of these twelve department heads has control of a certain function in soul or body. Each of these heads works through an aggregation of cells that physiology calls a "ganglionic center." Jesus, the I AM or central entity, has His throne in the top head, where phrenology locates spirituality. This is the mountain where He so often went to pray. The following outline gives a list of the Twelve, the faculties that they represent, and the nerve centers at which they preside:

Faith --- Peter -- center of brain.

Strength---Andrew --loins.

Discrimination or Judgment---James, son of Zebedee---pit of stomach.

Love---John---back of heart.

Power---Philip---root of tongue.

Imagination--Bartholomew--between the eyes.

Understanding ---Thomas--front brain.

Will ---Matthew--center front brain.

Order ---James, son of Alphaeus--navel.

Zeal --- Simon the Cananaean--back head, medulla.

Renunciation or Elimination --Thaddaeus--abdominal region.

Life Conserver---Judas--generative function.

The physiological designations of these faculties are not arbitrary--the names can be expanded or changed to suit a broader understanding of their full nature. For example, Philip, at the root of the tongue, governs taste; he also controls the action of the larynx, as well as all vibrations of power throughout the organism. So, the term "power" expresses but a small part of his official capacity.

The first apostle that Yeshua called was Peter. Peter represents faith in things spiritual, faith in God. We begin our religious experience, our unity with Divine Mind, by having faith in that mind as omnipresent, all-wise, all-loving, all-powerful Spirit.

Faith in the spiritual man quickens spiritual understanding. Peter believed that Jesus was the Messiah; his faith opened his spiritual discernment, and he saw the living Christ back of the personal mask worn by Yeshua. When asked, "Who do men say that the Son of man is?" the apostles, looking upon personality as the real, said: "Some say John the Baptist; some, Elijah; and others, Jeremiah, or one of the prophets." Then Jesus appealed to their own inner spiritual understanding and He said: "But who say ye that I am?" Only Simon Peter answered: "Thou art the Christ, the Son of the living God." And Jesus answered, "Thou art Peter, and upon this rock I will build my church, and the gates of Hades [the grave] shall not prevail against it. I will give unto thee the keys of the kingdom of heaven."

Spiritual discernment of the reality of man's origin and being is the only enduring foundation of character. It was to this faith in the understanding of the real being of man that Jesus gave power in earth and heaven. It was not to the personal Peter that Jesus gave the keys to His kingdom, but to all who through faith apply the binding (affirming) and loosing (denying) power of Spirit in the earth (substance consciousness). Right here and now the great work of character-building is to be done, and whoever neglects present opportunities, looking forward to a future heaven for better conditions, is pulling right away from the kingdom of heaven within himself.

People who live wholly in the intellect deny that man can know anything about God, because they do not have quickened faith. The way to bring forth the God presence, to make oneself conscious of God, is to say: I have faith in God; I have faith in Spirit; I have faith in things invisible. Such affirmations of faith, such praise to the invisible God, the unknown God, will make God visible to the mind and will strengthen the faith faculty. Thus faith (Peter) is called and instructed spiritually.

When a center loses its power, it should be baptized by the word of Spirit. We are told in the Scriptures that Philip went down to Gaza ("the same is desert"), and there baptized a eunuch. Gaza means a "citadel of strength." It refers to the nerve center in the loins, where Andrew (strength) reigns. "Lo now, his strength is in his loins." Gaza is the physical throne of strength, as Jerusalem is the throne of love.

The back grows weak under the burden of material thought. If you are given to pains in your back, if you become exhausted easily, you may know at once that you need treatment for freedom from material burdens. Eliminate from your mind all thought of the burdens of the world, the burdens of your life, and all seeming labors. Take your burdens to Christ. "Come unto me, all ye that labor and are heavy laden, and I will give you rest."

We are pressed upon by ideas of materiality. Thoughts make things, and the material ideas that are pressing upon us are just as substantial in the realm of mind as material things are substantial in the realm of matter.

Everything has origin in thought, and material thoughts will bring forth material things. So, you should baptize and cleanse with your spiritual word every center, as Philip baptized the eunuch of Gaza. Baptism is cleansing. It always represents the erasing power of the mind.

When the baptizing power of the word is poured upon a center, it cleanses all material thought; impotence is vitalized with new life, and the whole subconsciousness is awakened and quickened. The word of the Lord is there sown in the body, and once the word of the Lord is sown in any of these centers--the cells of which are like blank phonograph records--they take the thought that is given them and send it through the whole organism. The baptism of strength goes to the uttermost parts of the body, and every one of the twelve powers, under the divine law, feels the new strength.

James, the son of Zebedee, represents discrimination and good judgment in dealing with substantial things. James is the faculty in man that wisely chooses and determines. It may be in the matter of food; it may be in the matter of judgment about the relation of external forces; it may be in the choosing of a wife or a husband--in a thousand different ways this faculty is developed in man. The spiritual side of the James faculty is intuition, quick knowing.

James and John are brothers, and Jesus called them "sons of thunder." These brothers preside over the great body brain called the solar plexus, or sun center. James has his throne at the pit of the stomach; and John, just back of the heart. They are unified by bundles of nerves and are metaphysically closely related. Whatever affects the stomach will sympathetically affect the heart. People with weak stomachs nearly always think they have heart trouble.

Yeshua called those two apostles "sons of thunder." Tremendous vibrations or emotions that go forth from the solar plexus. When your sympathies are aroused, you will find that you begin to breathe deeply and strongly, and if you are very sympathetic you can feel the vibrations as they go out to the person or thing to which you are directing your thoughts. All fervor, all the high energy that comes from soul, passes through these centers.

Bartholomew represents the imagination. The imagination has its center of action directly between the eyes. This is the point of expression for a set of tissues that extend back into the brain and connect with an imaging or picture-making function near the root of the optic nerve. Through this faculty you can project an image of things that are without, or ideas that are within. For instance, you can project the image of jealousy to any part of your body and, by the chemistry of thought combined with function, make your complexion yellow, or you can image and project beauty by thinking goodness and perfection for everybody. Bartholomew is connected directly with the soul and has great power in the pictures of the mind. Jesus saw him under a fig tree, a long way off, before he was visible to the natural eye. Do not imagine anything but good, because under the law of thought combined with substance it will sooner or later come into expression, unless you head it off, eliminate it by denial.

Man has faculties of elimination, as well as of appropriation. If you know how to handle them you can expel error from your thought body. The denial apostle is Thaddaeus, presiding in the abdominal region, the great renunciator of the mind and the body. All the faculties are necessary to the perfect expression of the man. None is despised or unclean. Some have been misunderstood; through ignorance man has called them mean, until they act in that way and cause him pain and sorrow. The elimination, by Thaddaeus, of the waste of the system through the bowels is a very necessary function.

Thomas represents the understanding power of man. He is called the doubter because he wants to know about everything. Thomas is in the front brain, and his collaborator, Matthew, the will, occupies the same brain area. These two faculties are jointly in occupation of this part of the "promised land." Like the land of Ephraim and Manasseh, their inheritance in undivided.

James, the son of Alphaeus, represents divine order. His center is at the navel.

Simon, the Cananaean, represents zeal; his center is at the medulla, at the base of the brain. When you burn with zeal and are anxious to accomplish great things, you generate heat at the base of your brain. If this condition is not balanced by the co-operation of the supplying faculties, you will burn up the cells and impede the growth of the soul. "For the zeal of thy house hath eaten me up."

Judas, who betrayed Jesus, has his throne in the generative center. Judas governs the life consciousness in the body, and without his wise cooperation the organism loses its essential substance and dies. Judas is selfish; greed is his "devil." Judas governs the subtlest of the "beasts of the field"--sensation; but Judas can be redeemed. The Judas function generates the life of the body. We need life, but life must be guided in divine ways. There must be a righteous expression of life. Judas, the betrayer of Jesus, must in the end be cleansed of the devil, selfishness; having been cleansed, he will allow the life force to flow to every part of the organism. Instead of being a thief (drawing to the sex center the vital forces necessary to the substance of the whole man) Judas will become a supplier; he will give his life to every faculty. In the prevailing race consciousness Judas drains the whole man, and the body dies as a result of his selfish thievery.

It is through Judas (the desire to appropriate and to experience the pleasure of sensation) that the soul (Eve) is led into sin. Through the sins of the sex life (casting away of the precious substance), the body is robbed of its essential fluids and eventually disintegrates. The result is called death, which is the great and last enemy to be overcome by man. Immortality in the body is possible to man only when he has overcome the weaknesses of sensation and conserves his life substance. When we awaken to the realization that all indulgence for pleasure alone is followed by pain, then we shall know the meaning of eating of the tree of the knowledge of good and evil, or pleasure and pain.

If you would build up your faculties under the divine law, redeem Judas. First have faith in the power of Spirit, and then speak to Judas the word of purity. Speak to him the word of unselfishness; baptize him with the whole Spirit--Holy Spirit. If there is in you a selfish desire to exercise sensation, to experience the pleasures of sense in any of its avenues, give that desire to the Lord; in no other way can you come into eternal life.

These twelve powers are all expressed and developed under the guidance of Divine Mind. "Not by might, nor by power, but by my Spirit, saith Jehovah of hosts." You must keep the equipoise; you must, in all the bringing forth of the twelve powers of man, realize that they come from God: that they are directed by the Word of God, and that man (Jesus) is their head.

(B) The 12 apostles (heavenly)

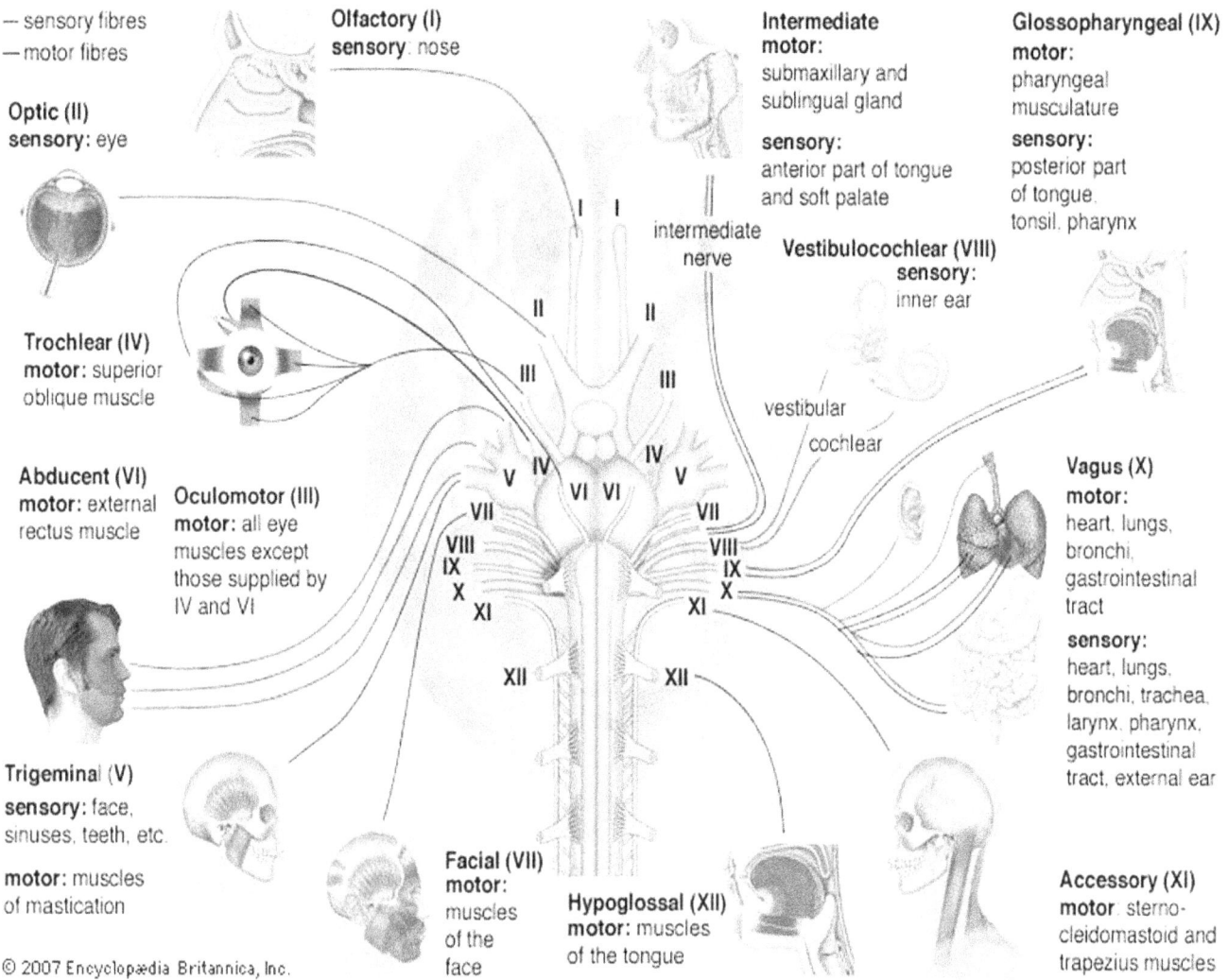

13ᵀᴴ CRANIAL NERVE

* Known as cranial nerve zero or Terminal Nerve
* It projects from nasal cavity, enters brain just a little bit ahead of other cranial nerves as a microscopic plexus of unmyelinated peripheral nerve fascicles

*13 is the vibration of new beginnings and thus, higher initiation into the universal/galactic mysteries of self.

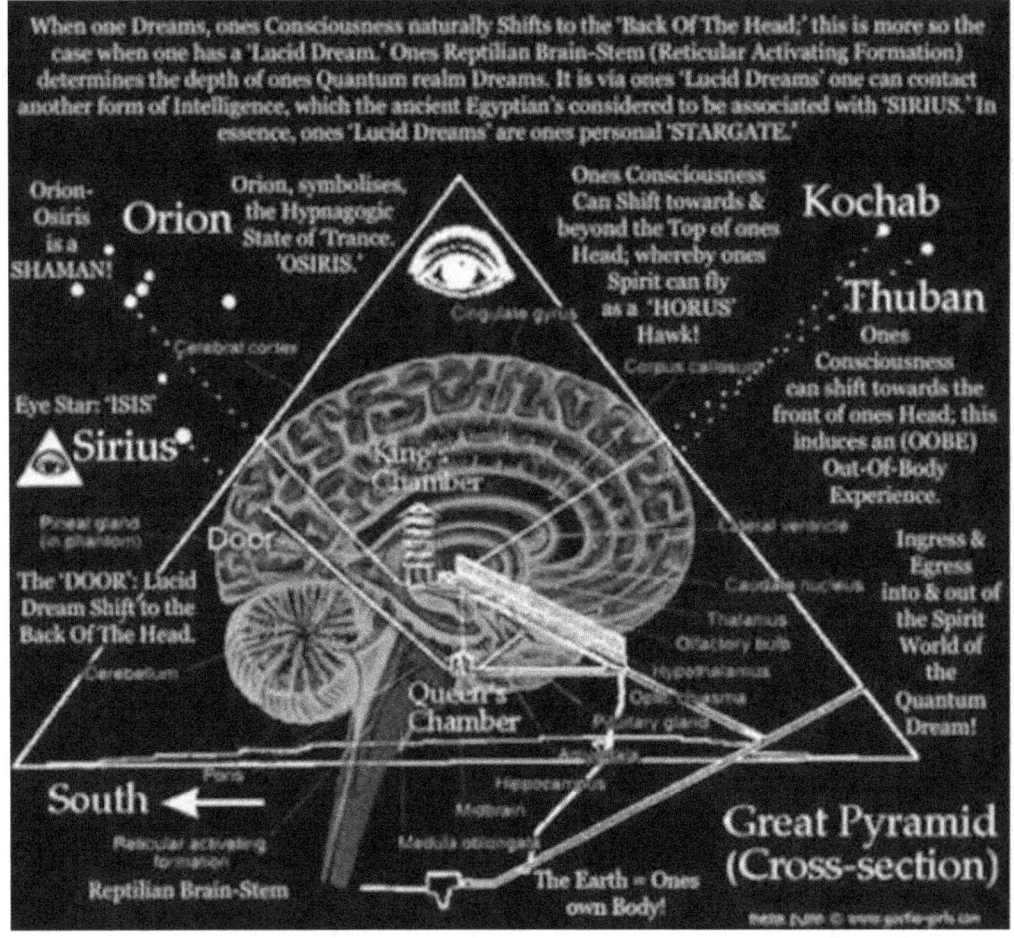

Luke 22:12-He will show you a large room upstairs, all furnished. Make preparations there.

(C) 12 Ideals of perfected man (earthly)

- Obedience-Aries
- Modesty-Taurus
- Gratitude-Gemini
- Charity-Cancer
- Temperance-Leo
- Prudence-Virgo
- Justice-Libra
- Sincerity-Scorpio
- Diligence-Sagittarius
- Benevolence-Capricorn
- Science-Aquarius
- Religion-Pisces

Social Houses
Motivated by Approval of Public

Personal Houses
Motivated by Personal Satisfaction

Gates
- **South Gate** — Objective
- **West Gate** — Dependent — Molded and influenced by Circumstances
- **North Gate** — Subjective
- **East Gate** — Independent — Molds and Creates Circumstances

Signs (clockwise from top)
Capricorn, Sagittarius, Scorpio, Libra, Virgo, Leo, Cancer, Gemini, Taurus, Aries, Pisces, Aquarius

Quadrant Labels
- Wealth / Fire (top)
- Relations / Endings (upper sides)
- Endings / Wealth (middle sides)
- Fire / Fire (lower sides)
- Wealth / Endings / Relations (bottom)

Houses (1–12) with Keywords
- 1 — Self
- 2 — Possessions / Finance
- 3 — Common Knowledge
- 4 — Self Origins
- 5 — How Spend Finance
- 6 — Application of Knowledge
- 7 — Other Than Self
- 8 — Reserves
- 9 — Higher Knowledge
- 10 — Others See Your Self
- 11 — How Hope To Spend
- 12 — Perfect Knowledge

115

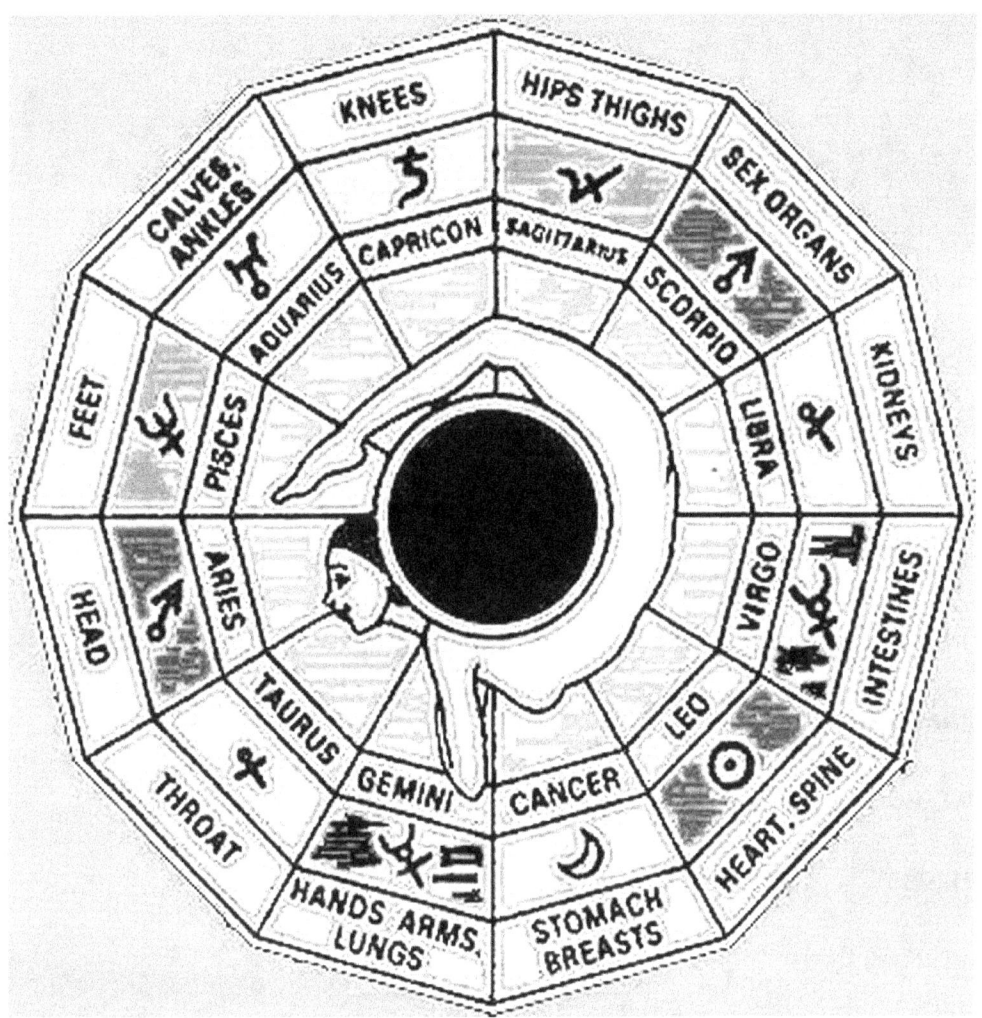

Chapter 5: The 7's

(A) The 7 chakras

Ezekiel 1: 16, 19-21: (16) The appearance of the wheels and their work was like unto the color of a beryl: and they four had one likeness: and their appearance and their work was as if it were a wheel in the middle of a wheel. (19) And when the living creatures went, the wheels went by them: and when the living creatures were lifted up from the earth, the wheels were lifted up. (20) Whithersoever the spirit was to go, they went, thither was their spirit to go; and the wheels were lifted up over against them: for the spirit of the living creature was in the wheels. (21) When those went, these went; and when those stood, these stood; and when those were lifted up from the earth, the wheels were lifted up over against them: for the spirit of the living creature was in the wheels.

(1) THE ROOT CHAKRA

SURVIVAL & SECURITY
Muladhara (moo-lahd-HA-rah)

Location: Perineum (between the anus and the genitals)

Primary Color: Red

Secondary Colors: Mauve, Brown

Right: To Have

Planets: Saturn & Earth

Element: Earth

Sense: Smell

Sound: Bb Note/Lam

Frequencies (Hz): 228, 456, 912

Shape/Number: Cube/4

Body: Skeletal system, teeth, large intestine, immune system, kidneys, blood, feet, hips, anus

Endocrine Gland: Gonads/Reproductive Glands- In men these are the testes which govern testosterone. In women they are the ovaries which release estrogen and progesterone. They control sexual development.

Balanced/Open Chakra: When the root chakra is balanced, one feels grounded, stable, and secure. You feel present in the here and now and feel connected to your physical body. You are energized, and daily tasks are done with ease. You have no doubt about your place in the world.

Underactive: An underactive root chakra will leave you feeling fearful and disconnected from the world and your body. The world and life around you make you feel nervous and anxious. You feel uneasy and unwelcome. You may feel disorganized and lack focus and discipline. You will lack in energy and desire to want to do anything or want anything out of life. You may also suffer from depression. Sex drive may be low.

Overactive: An overactive root chakra will make you feel angry, annoyed, and aggressive towards people and things in life. You tend to have a hard time accepting change and the flow of life. You may be obsessed with controlling others or their environment and feel threatened at anyone or anything that challenges your "authority". You will seek security in external things such as people, jobs, objects, or particular habits. You seek value and self-worth in material things and will feel insecure without them. Sex drive may be high.

Physical Symptoms: weight instability, anorexia, obesity, over/under active sex drive, poor immune system, anemia, depression, fatigue, arthritis, irritable bowel syndrome, prostate cancer, fibroids, uterine cancer.

The Root Chakra is the first most important chakra to balance. Balancing the root chakra builds a solid foundation for opening and balancing the rest of the 6 chakras. Like the foundation of a house, if it is weak the house cannot stand. The root chakra represents your ability to release energy, its position being near the anus (where wastes leave your body) and the perineum. When out of balance, the flow of energy is not being properly released and our connection to earth gets disconnected. The root chakra is also your survival center. It controls the fight or flight response, your primal and animal nature. This chakra also carries the energy of our parents and ancestors including their lessons, learned and unlearned, their triumphs and their challenges, and can create unconscious generational patterns. The root chakra can waver between underactive, balanced, and overactive at any given time, depending on situations, triggers, and how someone chooses to handle their fears and situations around them. The root chakra is the first to develop from birth to the age of 7. This developmental stage involves learning to trust and having our basic needs met such as food, water, shelter, protection and safety, which help you feel grounded and secure. However, if there were a series of events that left a child feeling unsafe, scared, or insecure, they tend to have root chakra imbalances that build fears and anxieties when it comes to facing the world, interactions with people, relationships, and even everyday activities. We will find ourselves repeating the same patterns we learned in childhood until those energies are uprooted to be resolved. "What you suppress, you will repeat." So, it is important to heal root chakra and subconscious issues.

How to Balance

The root chakra can be balanced with effort, physically and energetically, which will facilitate what needs to come up and be uprooted for spiritual healing.

1. Visualize the root chakra symbol and/or a bright red ball of light at the base of the perineum where the root chakra is positioned.
2. Stand in the grass barefoot for a few minutes, earth underneath your feet, allowing yourself to feel grounded to the earth and in the present moment.
3. Wear/carry root chakra crystals that best fit your needs.
4. Light a red candle to use during visualization and meditation.
5. Use aromatherapy with essential oils that have wood earthy scents. GROUNDING Root Chakra crystal infused oil is formulated to facilitate balance.
6. Listen to root chakra sound vibrations
7. Chant the seed of LAM in a note of Bb at the frequencies listed above that resonate with the 432 Hz chakra scale.
8. Wear the color red
9. Eat red colored foods and foods known to be roots such as ginger, carrots, beets, and eat high protein foods.
10. Practice root chakra yoga positions. In addition, these can be done in the grass barefoot for grounding.
11. Repeat root chakra affirmations daily.

Affirmations for Root Chakra Healing:
- I feel safe and secure
- I have what I need
- I am grounded
- I am connected to my body
- I am connected to the earth
- I accept things that help me grow and evolve
- I trust myself
- I am strong
- I am protected

- I am loved
- I release pain and negative energy

Root Chakra Crystals:

Black Tourmaline, Red Jasper, Snowflake Obsidian, Bloodstone, Hematite, Ruby, Brecciated Jasper, Red Tiger's Eye, Black Onyx, Garnet, Rainbow Obsidian, Smoky Quartz, Mookaite Jasper

(2) THE SACRAL CHAKRA

Creativity & Sexual Expression
Svadisthana (SWAH-dis-TAN-uh)

Location: Below the Navel

Primary Color: Orange

Secondary Colors: Gold, Amber

Right: To Act

Planet: Jupiter

Element: Water

Sense: Taste

Sound: Eb Note/Vam

Frequencies (Hz): 303, 606, 1212

Shape/Number: Icosahedron/6

Body: Sexual organs, prostate, womb, spleen, bladder, gallbladder, bowels, lower intestines, lower back

Endocrine Gland: Gonads- regulates sexual function and hormones. Adrenal glands- regulates metabolism and immune system in response to stress. Executes the "fight or flight" syndrome. Controls heart rate, breathing, blood pressure, decrease in the flow of blood to and function of organs not involved in the emergency response.

Balanced/Open Chakra: When the sacral chakra is balanced your emotions are able to flow freely and you can express them fully without being over-emotional. You radiate warmth and friendliness naturally to others within balance. You are open to intimacy and being passionate. You have a healthy and open expression of your sexuality. You feel confident and experience pleasure, joy, and abundance. You are able to let go, move on, accept change and transformation within the body, and experience the moment as is. You want to live and experience life to the fullest.

Underactive: An underactive sacral chakra will lead to being emotionally unattached, distant, or cold and you are not very open to people. You may have a flat or poker-faced expression. You will lack trueness of self, creativity and originality and "fitting in" is the main motivation. You feel as if you aren't good enough. You may express a fear of pleasure, denying yourself things that make you feel good, or things you really want and will make excuses of why you shouldn't or aren't deserving of them. You may also experience a weak or low sex drive.

Overactive: If you have an overactive sacral chakra, you will be overemotional and dramatic over people, situations, and events. You may come off as clingy and emotionally co-dependent. You constantly let the actions and approval of others control and rule your emotional outcome. You may also experience an over-active sex drive, feeling the need to have sex to fulfill emptiness and void or to satisfy emotional cravings.

Physical Symptoms: Bladder issues such as UTI's, kidney stones, gallbladder stones, vaginal cancers, irregular menstruation, ovarian cysts, endometriosis, pre-menstrual syndrome, infertility, prostate cancer, low sperm count.

The Sacral Chakra is the dwelling place of the self, constantly creating a new you in growth. It is the chakra responsible for the will to procreate. As children we experienced the world in our own creative way. There was no right or wrong way to do things, we just acted out of our own free flowing creativity. It isn't until we are taught the 'perceived' right or wrong way to do something that we become self-conscious about our originality and creative processes. As we get older, we begin to experience societal conditioning where we learn our feelings are not valued and passion and emotional reactions receive harsh criticism. We are taught what is "beautiful" or accepted and what is not and leaves us constantly comparing and judging ourselves to societal standards. We may have received rejection of some sort for showing our true self, or even liking someone. On a sexual level, this world is full of mixed signals about "healthy or unhealthy" sexual behaviors either being magnified and glorified or rejected and put to shame. With a mix of these experiences you may find yourself going along to just fit in, abandoning your true self and creative ideas. Open yourself to love your body without comparison. Experience your sexual self without shame or guilt. Let go of the fear of being judged. Remember how good it felt when you were being original, unique, and different. Become confident in yourself and your originality. Unplug yourself from the mainstream thinking. Accept yourself for who you are and let that grow.

How to Balance

1. Visualize the Sacral chakra symbol and/or a bright orange ball of light just below the navel where the sacral chakra is positioned.

2. Wear/carry sacral chakra crystals that best fit your needs during meditation and/or everyday use.

3. Light an orange candle to use during visualization or meditation.

4. Dance to some of your favorite music behind closed doors like no one is watching and enjoy the moment.

5. Be open to allowing yourself to be creative in ways such as drawing, writing, cooking, whatever suits you, without the care or concern of others.

6. Use aromatherapy with essential oils that have a flowery and/or sensual scent. PASSION Sacral Chakra crystal infused oil is formulated to facilitate balance.

7. Listen to sacral chakra sound vibrations

8. Chant the seed of VAM in the note of Eb by the frequencies listed above based on 432 Hz chakra frequencies.

9. Wear or surround yourself in the color orange.

10. Eat sacral balancing foods. Sweet fruit such as oranges, mangos, melons, and strawberries, nuts such as almonds, and use spices of vanilla and cinnamon.

11. Practice sacral chakra yoga positions.

12. Repeat sacral chakra affirmations.

Affirmations for the Sacral Chakra

- I am creative
- I love my body
- I value myself
- I am open to experiencing the moment
- I allow myself to experience pleasure
- My sexuality is sacred
- I am at peace

Sacral Chakra Crystals:
Carnelian, Moonstone, Orange Calcite, Tiger's Eye, Mookaite Jasper

(3) THE SOLAR PLEXUS CHAKRA

POWER & SELF - CONTROL
Manipura (MAN-ee-Poo-rah)

Location: Just above the navel, below the ribs

Primary Color: Yellow

Secondary Color: Gold

Right: To Act

Planet: Mars

Element: Fire

Sense: Sight

Note/Sound: F# Note/Ram

Frequencies (Hz): 182, 364, 728

Shape/Number: Tetrahedron/10

Body: Liver, gallbladder, stomach, upper intestines Endocrine: Adrenals-breaks down protein and lipids to produce glucose. Reduce inflammation and immune response. Controls the 'fight or flight' response to stress. Pancreas- (Alpha cells) produces glucagon responsible for raising blood glucose levels and triggers muscle and liver cells to break down glycogen to release glucose in the blood stream. (Beta cells) produces insulin responsible for lowering blood glucose levels after a meal. This triggers the absorption of glucose from the blood to the cells where it is stored.

Balanced/Open Chakra: When your solar plexus chakra is balance, you feel confident and powerful and have high self-esteem. You value yourself and your works and you feel as if you have purpose in everything you do. You carry strength and power in the ability to move forward and make conscious decisions in doing so. You are in complete control of your emotions and actions and the ego does not influence your actions. You have clear goal, intentions, and desires and are self-motivated. You naturally express yourself in a powerful way with the freedom to choose and direct your life. You have a good perception of who you are. You accept your place in the universe and accept and appreciate the positions people have in your life and acknowledge their uniqueness. You radiate with life energy.

Underactive: If your solar plexus chakra is underactive you may be very passive and indecisive. You doubt yourself and your decisions, usually ruled by being unconfident, or worried about what others will think of you. You often feel as though you are not good enough and seek constant approval from others. You tend to mistrust people or put your trust in the wrong people. You develop codependent relationships. You are often afraid to be alone. You are afraid to face or analyze thoughts or feelings and avoid feelings of depression and anxiety.

Overactive: If your solar plexus chakra is overactive you tend to be domineering. You are harsh, judgmental, and critical towards others and yourself. You are very rigid in your thinking and tend to easily find fault in things and people. You have a stubborn attitude, your way or no way, and may always think you are right. You may find yourself making plans but not fulfilling them. You tend to be a workaholic and work is the main priority. You are constantly working at perfecting things for feeling that nothing is ever good enough as it is.

Physical symptoms: Diabetes, digestive issues, adrenal organ illness, hypoglycemia, hyperglycemia, poor digestion, weight problems, ulcers, arthritis, issues with pancreas, liver and/or kidneys, hepatitis, colon cancer.

The Solar Plexus Chakra houses our will-power, the warrior within. It is the seat of fire, passion and desire, and the will to live. This chakra enables us to empower ourselves which helps us to open new doors in our life. When balanced there is no need to control another's will and neither are you wanting or needing to be controlled. It also helps us to overcome fears that control our lives. It teaches us how to balance the ego, self-confidence, and have self-control. In addition, the message this chakra carries, is that you have the POWER to choose. The power of choice is one of the greatest gifts in life. You can choose if you want to take charge and direction in your life. You can choose to live out your karma or actively make a decision to change it. You can choose healing. You can choose in this very moment if you want to smile or frown. Any time you judge or criticize yourself, you deplete this chakra and weaken your willpower. Loving yourself and knowing your value and your worth, that you are unique and one of a kind, are ways to build your solar plexus chakra. Know that you can express yourself in a powerful way and that you have the freedom to choose to be yourself and direct your own life. Stand firm in your own personal power.

How to Balance

1. Visualize the Solar Plexus chakra symbol and a bright yellow ball of light above the navel and below the rib cage where the solar plexus chakra is positioned.

2. Sit and bask in sunlight.

3. Wear/carry solar plexus chakra crystals that best fit your needs during meditation and/or everyday use.

4. Light a yellow candle to use during visualization or meditation. Concentrate on watching the movement and dance of the fire, imagining yourself being that light.

5. Stimulate your mind by playing mind puzzles, take a class in a field you enjoy doing, and by reading books. Completing or accomplishing these tasks builds strength and self-confidence.

6. Practice letting go of the ego and titles, and experience things as they are and as they come without the need to control it.

7. Use aromatherapy with essential oils that have a citrus or spicy scent. CONFIDENCE Solar Plexus Chakra crystal infused oil is formulated to facilitate balance.

8. Listen to solar plexus chakra sound frequency at a 432 Hz frequency calibration. This can also be used to clear energy from crystals. Just place corresponding crystals nearby as you play.

9. Chant the seed of RAM in the note of F# at the 432Hz frequency calibration

10. Wear or surround yourself in the color yellow.

11. Eat solar plexus balancing foods such as bananas, granola, grains, bread, flax seed, sunflower seeds and organic dairy such as cheese and yogurt. You can also incorporate certain herbs and spices such as ginger, turmeric, cumin, fennel, mint, and chamomile.

12. Practice solar plexus chakra yoga positions.

13. Repeat sacral chakra affirmations.

Affirmations for the Solar Plexus Chakra:

- I love myself
- I accept myself for who I am
- I release my ego(s)
- I am strong
- I am powerful
- I am proud of what I have achieved in life
- I am authentic
- I direct my own life
- I seek opportunities for personal and spiritual growth
- I am at peace with myself

Solar Plexus Crystals:
Citrine, Tiger's Eye, Rutilated Quartz, Ametrine

(4) THE HEART CHAKRA

COMPASSION & FORGIVENESS
Anahata (ah-NAH-hah-tah)

Location: Heart/Center of chest

Color: Green

Secondary Color: Pink

Right: To Love

Planets: Venus

Element: Air

Sense: Touch

Shape/Number: Octahedron/12

Note/Sound: C/Yam

Frequencies (Hz): 128, 256, 512

Endocrine Gland: Thymus-produces T-lymphocytes that protect a person from pathogens from birth and for the rest of their life.

Body: Heart, lungs, circulatory system, immune system, arms, and hands

Balanced/Open Chakra: When your heart chakra is balanced you have a love for yourself and understand that you must love yourself to love others. You have compassion for all things around you. You are open to feeling compassion for others and people feel at peace around you. You accept others for who they are. You are forgiving with the understanding that everyone has their own process. You aren't critical or judgmental but rather nurturing. You radiate unconditional love. You share deep bonds with others. You are kind, caring, joyous, and at peace.

Underactive: When your heart chakra is underactive you find it hard to give or receive love and seem distant and cold. You are very protective of your feelings. You usually think negatively towards people and things. You have a hard time having a positive outlook on life. You feel unloved and unappreciated from others and self. It's hard for you to believe others can be compassionate and you may shut down from the ability to heal for fear of being hurt.

Overactive: When you heart chakra is overactive you love with conditions. Loving someone is mostly about your own wants and desires. You may be manipulative. You make decisions and are ruled by grief, anger, sadness, resentment, despair, and/or greed and may find yourself cycling in hurtful patterns. You tend to form codependent relationships and have a hard time letting go of situations that no longer serve any higher good. You are a people pleaser, always giving and most likely not receiving for fear of being disliked or unloved.

Physical Symptoms: Heart problems, high blood pressure, high cholesterol, heart murmurs, congestive heart failure, heart attack, stroke, blood issues, anemia, leukemia, pneumonia, bronchitis, flu, excess mucus, emphysema, asthma, lung cancer, breast cancer.

The Heart Chakra governs our ability to love self and others, be forgiving, compassionate and move through hurt and pain. It opens us to generosity, altruism, selflessness, kindness, and respect. The heart chakra is the source of wholeness and healing- love is the ultimate force of healing. One of the most important qualities about this chakra is that it is the connector or bridge between the lower three chakras, the material, and the upper three chakras, the spiritual. It represents the balance. It stimulates the flow of energy and is an important factor in chakra health. This chakra being off balance is a large contributor to the number one killers such as blood pressure, heart attack, stroke, and breast cancer. Holding on to grief and anger is a lead to these illnesses.

Everyone has experienced hurt at some point in their life, either by parents, friends, or a significant other, or by a loss they have encountered. It's almost impossible to avoid being hurt, but how you handle such grievances can make the difference between a closed or open chakra. You can choose to let go of anger and grief with the understanding that things people seem to do to hurt us are not always personal, but an extension of their own pain experienced before you. "Hurt people hurt people". Being open to this understanding opens you to compassion, love, and understanding, which opens your heart to new experiences and new people. Holding on to hurt and negative feelings blocks you from opportunities to love and you will find yourself "stuck" until you accept those feelings and let them go.

To learn to have empathy and compassion for someone else is allowing yourself to walk in their shoes, experiencing a circumstance the way they would have. It is taking your personal feelings out of a situation and understanding it from a point of view other than your own. Yet when someone has hurt us or offended us, it becomes hard to do. However, everyone has a story that has made them the way they are. Learn to forgive and move on from painful situations in your life. To receive love, you must learn to give love. Simple things you can do to give love; smile at everyone you see. A genuine smile from a stranger can do so much to a person having a bad day. Let go of grudges, life is too short. Give friends positive affirmations and feedback. Learn how not to criticize others including yourself. Learn and grow through painful experiences and be compassionate towards others suffering.

How to Balance

1. Visualize the heart chakra symbol (at top) and/or a bright green ball of light centered in the middle of the chest where the heart chakra is located.

2. Wear or carry heart chakra crystals that best fit your needs during meditation and everyday use.

3. Light a green candle to use during visualization, meditation, or daily use.

4. Sit outside and breathe in fresh air. Enjoy the breeze of air dancing on your skin and around you. Take a nature scenic walk.

5. Think loving and positive thoughts. Anytime your mind tries to create something negative, replace it with a loving thought.

6. Use aroma therapy with essential oils. LOVE Heart Chakra crystal infused oil is formulated to facilitate heart chakra balance.

7. Listen to heart chakra sound frequencies. These can also be used to balance and clear crystals. Play and place the corresponding crystals nearby.

8. Chant the seed of YAM in the note of C with a 432 Hz frequency calibration.

9. Wear or surround yourself with the color green.

10. Eat heart balancing foods. Leafy green vegetables such as kale, spinach, and lettuce help keep the heart chakra system healthy. You can also incorporate other foods and herbs such as squash, celery, cabbage, basil, thyme, sage, parsley, and cilantro to name a few.

11. Practice heart chakra yoga positions.

12. Repeat heart chakra affirmations.

Affirmations for the Heart Chakra:

- I love myself
- I am worthy of love
- I open myself to forgive others that hurt me
- I am open to loving others unconditionally
- I forgive myself
- I am loved
- I open myself to receive love
- I allow healing into my heart
- I let go of pain and grief
- I let go of anger
- I let go of grudges
- I accept moving forward
- I am a source of healing in the world

Heart Chakra Crystals:
Rose Quartz, Bloodstone, Green Aventurine, Malachite, Jade, Peridot, Garnet, Serpentine, Unakite, Amazonite

(5) THE THROAT CHAKRA

Communication & Self-Expression
Vishuddha (vee-SHOO-duh)

Location: Neck (in the V)

Color: Blue

Secondary Colors: Silver, Turquoise

Right: To Express/Speak

Planets: Mercury

Element: Ether or Akasha

Sense: Hearing

Note/Sound: G Note/Ham

Frequencies (Hz): 192, 384, 768

Shape/Number: Dodecahedron/16

Body: Throat, thyroid, neck, mouth, teeth, tongue, jaw, ears

Endocrine Glands: *Thyroid*-releases calcitonin when calcium ion levels in the blood rise. Reduces amount of calcium in the blood. Releases hormones to regulate metabolic rate. *Parathyroid*-releases PTH hormone when calcium levels drop in the blood and also triggers the kidneys to return filtered calcium in the blood to be conserved.

Balanced/Open Chakra: When the throat chakra is balanced you are honest and not afraid to speak your personal truth. You express yourself creatively and assertively. You can say what you mean and remain tactful with your words. You are excellent at offering good sound advice to those that need it, even to yourself. You are usually upfront and not afraid to ask for what you want. You have no problems with voicing your weaknesses with the understanding of teaching others to grow and you are highly respected for it. You are able to transform negative experiences into wisdom and learning.

Underactive: When the throat chakra is underactive or closed it is difficult for you to express yourself. You feel misunderstood or misinterpreted which leaves you feeling isolated around others. You are afraid to speak your personal truth and formulate your words to please others by telling them what they want to hear. You may come across as being unreliable or "wishy-washy". Your life may be stagnant, and you may find yourself not getting what you want or situations not going your way. You may carry a lot of guilt.

Overactive: When the throat chakra is overactive, you tend to be over-opinionated and critical of others. You can be verbally abusive and yell excessively and unnecessarily. You may have very little tolerance for people's opinions. You don't allow others to talk back, it's your way or no way. You are judgmental for how people perform in life. You can be an excessive liar and/or a bad listener.

Physical Symptoms: Asthma, neck stiffness/pain, sore throat, problems with vocal cords, earaches, sinus infections, tonsillitis, laryngitis, thyroid cancer, hyperactive thyroid, teeth problems.

The Throat Chakra represents the valve for which all the chakras are expressed through. Especially for the first lower 5 chakras. The root and the sacral chakras dealing with overcoming fear and being secure, the solar plexus chakra being our seat of power and confidence, the heart chakra connecting to love and compassion, connect to help one express themselves in their light of truth. The imbalance of this chakra may be cause by events in a person's childhood. They may have grown up in an environment where they were not allowed to express themselves verbally, could have been constantly told to be quiet, judged for things that they said, and shut down for speaking their feelings. The process of communication between adult and child were highly unbalanced. Some children pick up lying habits that don't ever get fully corrected. Another scenario is that a person could be in a relationship, or friendships, and may be afraid to speak out for themselves and find themselves "going along just to get along", suppressing communication and their expression of truth. It can come from fear (root chakra), attachment (sacral chakra), lack of confidence (solar plexus chakra), and/or fear on not being loved or losing love (heart chakra). Guilt is another major reason this chakra becomes blocked.

It is important that we find our own truths and not be afraid to speak what we feel. There is a delicate balance to learn how to express oneself creatively, effectively, and tactfully. When this chakra is balanced, it allows us to seek knowledge beyond what we were taught to believe. It unblocks doubt and negative thinking and moves us into higher knowledge, thus accepting our own truth.

How to Balance

1. Visualize the throat chakra symbol (at top) and/or a bright blue light at the "V" area of your neck where your throat chakra is located.

2. Wear or carry throat chakra crystals that best fit your needs during meditation or everyday use. (See Crystal chart)

3. Light a blue candle to use during visualization, meditation, before a conversation with someone, or daily use.

4. Sing songs out loud. Try to practice speaking aloud to yourself. Talking to yourself is a way to be your own sounding board. You may uncover things about yourself that someone might otherwise judge. So be your own good listener. Be a good listener to others. Speak your true feelings to a trusted friend or therapist.

5. Use aromatherapy with essential oils that correspond to the throat chakra. EXPRESS Throat Chakra crystal infused oil is formulated with bright notes to facilitate throat chakra healing.

6. Listen to throat chakra sound frequencies. These can also be used to clear and balance crystals. Place the throat chakra crystals nearby as you play it.

7. Chant the seed of Ham in the note of G with a 432 Hz frequency calibration.

8. Eat foods that connect to this chakra such as lemons, grapefruit, lime, kiwi, apples, plums, pears, apricots, and peaches. You can also drink lots of water and herbal teas such as chamomile, peppermint, and Echinacea to name a few.

9. Practice throat chakra yoga positions

10. Repeat Throat chakra affirmations

Affirmations for the Throat Chakra:

- I speak with confidence

- I am open, clear, and honest in communication
- I am open to expressing my feelings creatively
- I speak tactfully

- I have a right to speak my truth

- I am strong willed and can resolve my challenges - I let go of any guilt

- I will not judge myself

- I am open to my truth

- I stand firm in my truth

Throat Chakra Crystals:

Kyanite, Lapis Lazuli, Sodalite, Aquamarine, Chrysocolla, Blue Lace Agate, Labradorite, Celestite, Amazonite

(6) THE THIRD - EYE CHAKRA

Intuition & Wisdom
Anja (UHN-jah)

Location: Brow (between the eyes)

Color: Indigo

Secondary Colors: Mauve, Turquoise

Right: To Perceive

Planet: Moon

Element: Light

Sense: 6th sense/Intuition

Sound: D Note/Aum (Om)

Frequencies (Hz): 144, 288, 576

Shape/Number: Merkaba/2

Body: Left eye, skull, brain, nervous system, the senses, pineal

Endocrine Gland: *Pineal gland*-produces melatonin that help regulate sleep-wake cycles called circadian rhythm. Increased levels of melatonin make one feel drowsy or in a dream-like state when the pineal gland is active.

Balanced/ Open Chakra: When the third-eye chakra is balanced you have a strong sense of intuition and perception beyond ordinary sight. You are connected to a different way of seeing and perceiving things. You may experience visions of things, de-ja-vu, and/or have prophetic and intuitive dreams. You are sensitive to subtle energies and vibrations of people, things, the atmosphere, etc. Wisdom is easily accessible. You able to rise above your emotions and see the bigger picture, understanding that life and situations have a deeper meaning. With this understanding you are open to receiving messages from the Universe. You are motivated inspirationally and creatively. You can have intuitive abilities such as clairvoyance (sight), clairaudience (hearing), clairsentience (feeling), claircognizance (knowing), clairgustance (tasting), and/or clairairalience (smelling). You are in-tuned with a higher source.

Underactive: If the third-eye chakra is underactive or closed, it is difficult for you to understand spiritual connections. You aren't connected to see how things spiritually relate. You aren't aware of signs and how they relate to you. You may feel confused and disconnected. You rely too much on your own beliefs and not open to new energy or information. You may have no intuition or have a hard time "tapping in". You may feel stuck and not able to look beyond your problems. You reject anything spiritual or out of the ordinary. You may not see the greater picture and lack a vision of clarity.

Overactive: If the third-eye chakra is overactive you tend to be overintellectual in thinking. You tend to be judgmental, over-logical, and unsympathetic. You may create circumstances in your mind that aren't happening. You aren't open to or even misinterpret spiritual information for logic and 'what makes sense'. You may fantasize too much and often have stress with headaches.

Physical Symptoms: Headaches, nightmares, bi-polar, glaucoma, neurological issues, brain cysts, tumors, strokes, blindness, deafness, seizures, insomnia, learning disabilities, panic, depression, addiction, migraines, sinus infections, earaches, hormonal imbalances.

The Third-Eye Chakra is connected to our sense of intuition, higher learning, and wisdom. It is the seat of conscience. You have the ability to see both inner and outer worlds when this chakra is healthy and open. It allows us a deeper perception of inner-reflection and helps us get a clear vision of ourselves as well as situations. If you can calm your mind in the midst of heightened emotions, you can receive messages that give you insight to a higher meaning. A lot of people have been taught that things they see aren't real or misinterpret or judge information they receive based on logic and judging their spiritually. Children are sensitive to energies until they are taught to "materialize" what they feel. However, when you understand that everything consists of energy and carries a vibration, you can start tuning in to feel those subtle frequencies. Black/white, good/bad, negative/positive are only extremes of the same energy. You must gain the ability to see things beyond what they are. It is understanding that everything happens for a reason and searching for the spiritual answers in everything. What are situations in your life meant to teach you? It takes detaching from situations, circumstances, material things, emotions, thought patterns, anything that leave you stuck in a box form of thinking. If you cannot DETACH then you stop the flow of intuition. Some people are more intuitive than others but with practice, tuning in, and learning life lessons, one's sense of intuition can be greatly increased.

How to Balance

1. Visualize the third-eye chakra symbol (at top) and/or a bright indigo colored ball of light in the center of the brow where the third eye chakra is located.

2. Wear or carry third-eye chakra crystal that best fit your balancing needs during meditation or everyday use. (See crystal chart)

3. Light indigo, dark blue (or purple) candles during meditation, or when trying to tune in or receive an intuitive answer about a situation.

4. Sitting in sunlight and detoxifying the body are great ways to boost the pineal gland and balance the third-eye chakra.

5. Use aromatherapy with essential oils that correspond to the third eye chakra. WISDOM Third-Eye Chakra crystal infused oil is formulated to facilitate balance.

6. Listen to third-eye chakra sound frequencies. This can also be used to cleanse and balance third-eye chakra crystals. Place your crystal nearby as you play it.

7. Chant the seed OM in the note of D with a 432 Hz frequency calibration.

8. Eat foods that are rich in omega-3 fatty acids such as fish and nuts. Eat vegetables and fruits rich in antioxidants such as blueberries. Dark chocolate is good as well.

9. Practice third-eye chakra yoga positions.

10. Repeat third-eye chakra affirmations.

Affirmations for the Third-Eye Chakra:

- I open myself to receive knowledge, wisdom, and information
- I am spiritually connected
- I am learning spiritual connections
- I listen to my intuition
- I open myself to be guided by my inner vision
- I am open to connecting to the Universal truth that lives inside of me
- I strive for higher understanding in all situations
- I cannot be fooled by illusions
- I clearly translate signs, symbols, and dreams

Third-Eye Chakra Crystals

Amethyst, Chevron Amethyst, Lapis Lazuli, Sodalite, Herkimer Diamond, Purple Fluorite, Moonstone

(7) THE CROWN CHAKRA

Higher Self & Enlightenment
Sahasrana (sah-has-SRA-nah)

Location: Top of the head/crown

Color: Violet

Secondary Color: White

Right: To Know

Planet: Sun

Element: Cosmic Energy

Sense: 7th sense

Sound: A Note/Silence

Frequencies (Hz): 216, 432, 864

Shape/Number: Sphere/1000

Body: Right eye, top of spinal cord, brain stem, nerves, pain center

Endocrine Glands: *Pineal gland*-regulates melanin and serotonin. *The pituitary gland*-the posterior: nervous tissue that releases oxytocin and ADH (antidiuretic hormone). Anterior: releases hormones to stimulate the thyroid and adrenal cortex. Also, hormones to stimulate follicle cells to produce gametes-ova in females, sperm in males. stimulates gonads to produce sex hormones estrogen and testosterone. Releases human growth hormone that stimulate cell growth, repair, and reproduction. Releases prolactin that stimulates milk production.

Balanced/Open Chakra: When the crown chakra is balanced, you are connected to your higher self and the Divine consciousness. You are spiritually aware that everything is interconnected and are able to experience the oneness with everyone and everything. You are able to transcend above the ego and manifest purpose from your higher self. Not only do you understand that everything happens for a reason, but you are open to receiving the answers of why. You are highly intuitive and gain great wisdom from your life experiences. You are selflessly devoted to the wellbeing of others and their spiritual health. You tend to be sensitive to energy and vibration. You trust the universal process and how it leads and guides your life.

Underactive: If your crown chakra is underactive or closed you feel like you lack purpose in life. You separate yourself from things and tend to have an "it's all meaningless" outlook on life. You may feel unloved or angry at "God" and constantly find things or people to blame outside of yourself. It's hard for you to grasp new ideas and you may feel a creative block. You tend to have a negative outlook on situations that have happened in your life. You have no desire to discover your inner-self or look for a higher purpose. You may feel or seem to others as clueless of anything spiritual. You tend to be clumsy, have poor balance, and co-ordination difficulties. You hold on to difficult things in life and they build and consume your way of thinking.

Overactive: If your crown chakra is overactive, you tend to be someone who may have a lot of knowledge but do not make the connections to process it as it relates to you on a deeper spiritual level. You may intellectualize things too much. You tend to possess a superior/god-complex and think that you are better than others. You have a hard time grounding yourself. Your ego stays ahead of you and you have a hard time letting things go because of it. Your judgements tend to be based solely on facts and you are not open to spiritual conclusions or explanations.

Physical Problems: Depression, senile dementia, Alzheimer's disease, Parkinson's disease, Schizophrenia, epilepsy, many other mental disorders, confusion, dizziness, muscular diseases, and sensitivity to light and sound.

The Crown Chakra is where our body makes the connection to the Universal Life Source. Many call this source God, Higher Power, the Divine, and the like. Through this chakra we experience unity with our higher selves and our divine purpose in life. It allows us to understand that there is a higher purpose in all things and that everything connects on deeper and spiritual levels.

The one factor that stops us from enlightenment is the ego. The ego is the being you perceive yourself to be, the illusion of oneself. The ego is the protective layer built from fear through experiences in our childhood, adolescence, and adulthood. It stems from the subconscious mind. The problem with the ego is that it separates itself from everything. It is constantly in competition, always wanting to be right and never wrong, and be in control of all things. It is the "I" consciousness and thinks only of self-preservation. The ego tends to be judgmental and because of this separatism fails to move into higher energies to understand things on a deeper and more connected level. It often personalizes events and holds on to everything building yet another layer. As you continue to allow the ego to grow, it becomes more challenging to let go of ideals and beliefs that we built to protect the ego, which weighs us down. The ego will label things, such as good or bad. It seeks things to satisfy itself and rejects things that don't. It leaves a person on a constant cycle and range of emotions, from highs and lows. The ego stops us from growing until it is broken and re-evaluated and humbled from the connection made through the higher self.

You must learn to recognize your ego self. It is not 'bad' but becomes a problem when it controls you and you think that your ego self is your true self. When you learn to recognize it, you can then work in harmony with it. There is a delicate balance between the ego and the higher self. It helps us to identify that we are different, unique, and individual, while the higher self keeps it humble enough to stay connected. You must question yourself and your motivations. Are they selfish or selfless? Are you showing your true self or a mask? To humble your ego, you must learn the art of detachment. You must detach from control, fears, pain, ideas, and beliefs. You must know that all things happen for a reason and as they should. The Universe does not make mistakes, it just is. You will then find peace and learn to trust the process thus allowing the exchange of energy from the Universe in through the crown chakra that resonates throughout the rest of the body and the other chakras.

How to Balance

To bring the Crown Chakra into balance, meditation and letting go of the ego are the first key steps.

1. Visualize the Crown chakra symbol and/or a bright white or purple light above the crown of your head.

2. Sit outside in nature and allow yourself to feel at one with all around you.

3. Wear/carry crown chakra crystals that best fit your needs.

4. Light a purple or white candle to use during the day, for visualization or meditation.

5. Use aromatherapy with essential oils. LIGHT Crown Chakra crystal infused oil is formulated to facilitate balance.

6. Listen to crown chakra vibrations (See below)

7. Quiet your mind and allow yourself to feel connected to your spirit and higher self. Concentrate on raising your vibration.

8. Wear white or purple.

9. Choose foods that are healthy and avoid processed foods. Consume less meat and other foods that have been chemically processed. Drinking lots of water and natural detoxing will help keep this chakra healthy.

10. Practice crown chakra yoga positions.

11. Repeat crown chakra affirmations daily.

Affirmations for the Crown Chakra:

- I trust my inner and higher self
- I connect myself to the Universe
- I let go of my ego
- I humble myself
- I understand that all things happen for a reason -- Everyone I meet is meant to teach me something, so I can grow
- I am balanced
- I am open to my higher consciousness
- I open myself to receive light

Crown Chakra Crystals:
Amethyst, Chevron Amethyst, Ametrine, Herkimer Diamond, Moonstone, Purple Fluorite, Clear Quartz, Selenite, Tourmalinated Quartz, Celestite

Revelation 5:1-Then I saw in the right hand of him who sat on the throne a scroll with writing on both sides and sealed with seven seals.

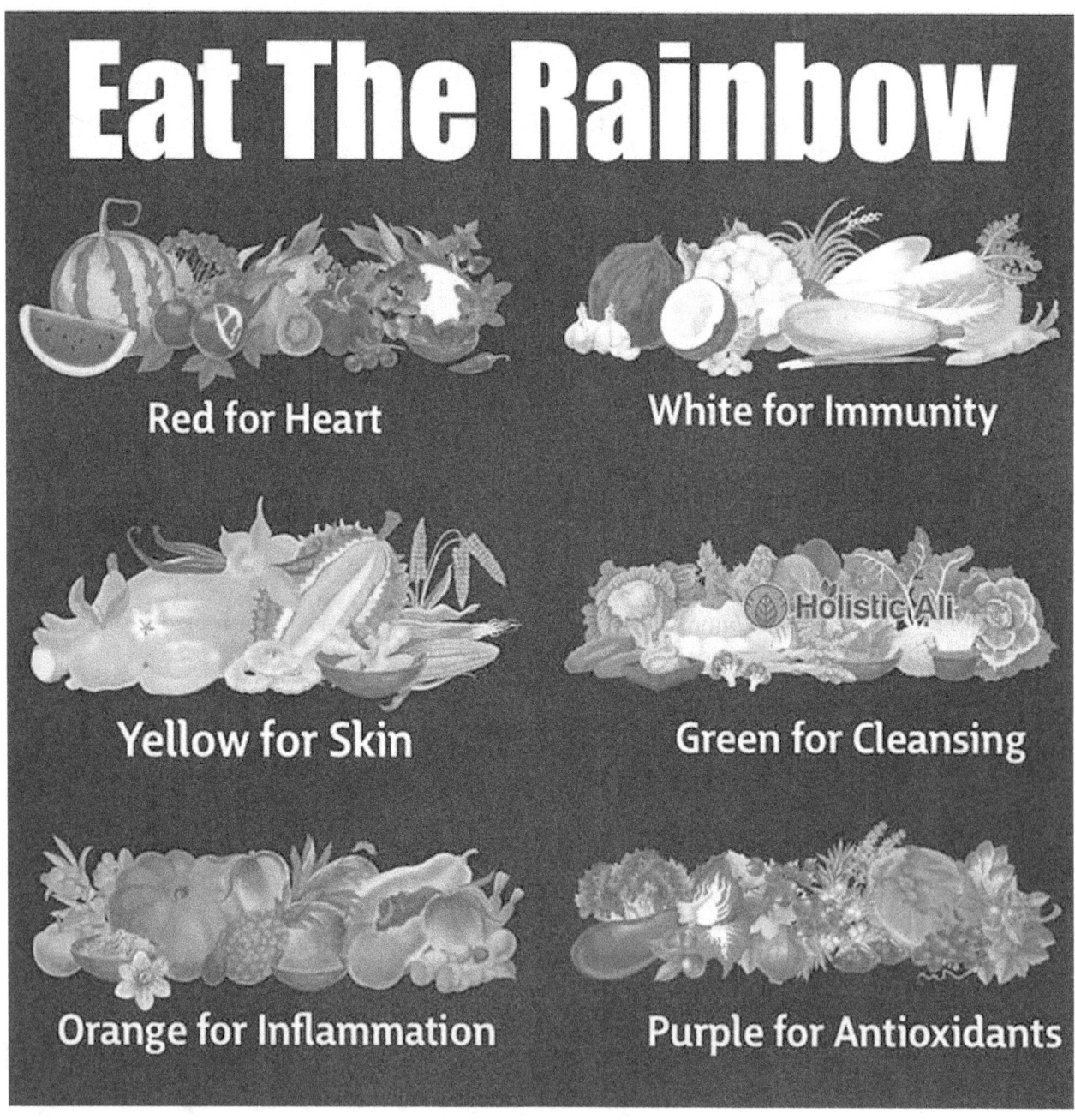

Eating in Biological RHYTHM

5-12 noon —  Fruits, herbs, and water to help the body flushes and cleanse out waste

12-3 pm —  Vegetables at noon to replenish the cells and feed the body minerals, chlorophyll, melanin, and carbon

3-8 pm —  In the evening more solid foods can be eating, but no eating after 8 pm

@doctorholistic

(B) The 7 spiritual laws

The Law of Pure Potentiality. The field of pure potentiality is the silent realm from which all things flow, from which "the unmanifest is made manifest". When we access it, we experience our higher, pure selves, and can see the futility and waste of living through the ego. While the ego is based in fear, the higher self exists in loving security: "It is immune to criticism, it is unfearful of any challenge, and it feels beneath no one." We can access the field of pure potentiality primarily through meditation and silence, but also through the practice of non-judgement and in appreciation of nature.

The Law of Giving. The more you give, the more you receive, and the author says that it's because our minds and bodies are in a constant state of giving and receiving with the universe. The more we give, the more we are involved in the circulation of the universe's energy, and the more of it we will receive back, in the form of love, material things, serendipitous experiences. We are never limited in what we can give because the true nature of man is one of affluence and abundance.

The Law of "karma" or Cause and Effect. Karma" is both action and the consequence of that action: every action generates a force of energy that returns to us in like kind. If we want to create happiness in our lives, we must learn to sow the seeds of happiness. Everything that is happening in our lives right now is a result of the choices we made in the past – only, most of them were made unconsciously, even it's only a matter of feelings: you can choose to be offended or not by an insult, that's also a choice. We should work on becoming aware of all of our choices.

The Law of Least Effort. It is human nature to turn our dreams into reality – with ease. Chopra follows The Vedic principle of economy of effort which says, "do less and accomplish more". He suggests that, when our actions are motivated by love, not the desires of the ego, we generate excess energy that can be used to create anything we want. The first step is to practice acceptance, because we cannot hope to channel the universe's effortless power if we are fighting against it.

The Law of Intention and Desire. While a tree is locked into a single purpose, the intelligence of the human nervous system allows us to actually shape the mind and the laws of nature to bring about the achievement of a desire that we have freely imagined. We can do that by using the processes of attention and intention: while attention on something will energize it and make it expand, intention triggers energy and information and "organizes its own fulfillment". Once the intention is introduced, we can "let the universe handle the details".

The Law of Detachment. We must give up our attachment to the realization of our intention before it can manifest, because if we are attached to a specific outcome it will produce fear and insecurity at the possibility of it not happening. When we're attached to an outcome, we feel we must force solutions onto problems; when we are detached from it, we are free to witness the perfect solutions that spontaneously emerge from chaos.

The law of "dharma" or Purpose in Life. There's a reason why we have taken manifestation in physical form – there's a purpose to fulfill. Each of us first has to discover our higher self or our spiritual self; then we need to express our unique talents, because there's something that no one in the world does better than us – our own talent; and third is to serve our fellow human beings and to ask our self the question "How can I help?"

(C) The 7 steps of manifestation

- Vision-visualize what you want.
- Desire-be intensely excited about what you are visualizing.
- Belief-believe what you desire is possible to manifest.
- Acceptance-accept your belief and your ability to manifest it as being true.
- Intent-want and intent are different. You must have the intention to manifest your desire.
- Action-act and behave like your desire has already manifested.
- Allowance-detach from the outcome. You have to be intense in your desire without any expectation that it manifest.

Chapter 6: The Art of Peace

"You cannot ask the darkness to leave; you must turn on the light." Sogyal Rinpoche

"However, many holy words you read, however many you speak, what good will they do if you do not act upon them." -Gautama Buddha

The Art of Peace begins with you. Work on yourself and your appointed task in the Art of Peace. Everyone has a spirit that can be refined, a body that can be trained in some manner, a suitable path to follow. You are here to realize your inner divinity and manifest your innate enlightenment. Foster peace in your own life and then apply the Art to all than you encounter.

The Way of the Warrior has been misunderstood. It is not a means to kill and destroy others. Those who seek to compete and better one another are making a terrible mistake. To smash, injure, or destroy is the worst thing a human being can do. The real Way of a Warrior is to prevent such slaughter — it is the Art of Peace, the power of love.

One does not need buildings, money, power, or status to practice the Art of Peace. Heaven is right where you are standing, and that is the place to train.

In the Art of Peace, we never attack. An attack is proof that one is out of control. Never run away from any kind of challenge, but do not try to suppress or control an opponent unnaturally. Let attackers come any way they like and then blend with them. Never chase after opponents. Redirect each attack and get firmly behind it.

Foster peace in your own life and then apply the Art to all that you encounter.

Your spirit is the true shield.

Instructors can impart only a fraction of the teaching. It is through your own devoted practice that the mysteries of the Art of Peace are brought to life.

Techniques employ four qualities that reflect the nature of our world. Depending on the circumstance, you should be: hard as a diamond, flexible as a willow, smooth-flowing like water, or as empty as space.

There are no contests in the Art of Peace. A true warrior is invincible because he or she contests with nothing. Defeat means to defeat the mind of contention that we harbor within.

When you bow deeply to the universe, it bows back; when you call out the name of God, it echoes inside you.

All things, material and spiritual, originate from on source and are related as if they were one unit. The past, present, and future are all contained in the life force. The universe emerged and developed from one source, and we evolved through the optimal process of unification and harmonization.

All sounds and vibrations emanate from that word. Your voice is a very powerful weapon. When you are in tune with the cosmic breath of heaven and earth, your voice produces true sounds. Unify body, mind, and speech, and real techniques emerge.

The art of peace emanated from the divine form and the divine heart of existence; it reflects the true good, beautiful, and absolute nature of creation and the essence of its ultimate grand design. The purpose of the art of peace is to fashion sincere human beings; a sincere human being is one who has unified body and spirit, one who is free of hesitation or doubt, and one who understands the power of words.

If you have life in you, you have access to the secrets of the ages, for the truth of the universe resides in each and every human being.

The art of peace is medicine for a sick world. We want to cure the world of the sickness of violence, malcontent, and discord-this is the way of harmony. There is evil and disorder in the world because people have forgotten that all things emanate from one source. Return to that source and leave behind all self-centered thoughts, petty desires, and anger.

Those who are possessed by nothing possess everything.

Practice of the art of peace is an act of faith, a belief in the ultimate power of nonviolence. It is faith in the power of purification and faith in the power of life itself. It is not a type of rigid discipline or empty asceticism. It is a path that follows natural principles, principles that must be applied to daily living. The art of peace should be practiced from the time you rise to greet the morning to the time you retire at night.

Inner principles give coherence to things; the art of peace is a method of uncovering those principles.

A good mixture is 70%e. faith and 30% science. Faith in the art of peace will allow you to understand the intricacies of modern science.

Conflict between material and spiritual science creates physical and mental exhaustion, but when matter and spirit are harmonized, all stress and fatigue disappear.

Use your body to create forms; use your spirit to transcend forms; unify body and spirit to activate the art of peace.

If you have not linked yourself to true emptiness, you will never understand the art of peace.

Eight forces sustain creation: movement and stillness, solidification and fluidity, extension and contraction, unification and division.

Life is growth. If we stop growing, technically and spiritually, we are as good as dead. The art of peace is a celebration of the bonding of heaven, earth, and humankind. It is all that is true, good, and beautiful.

Now and again, it is necessary to seclude yourself among deep mountains and hidden valleys to restore your link the source of life. Sit comfortably and first contemplate the manifest realm of existence. This realm is concerned with externals, the physical form of things. Then fill your body with Ki and sense the manner in which the universe functions, its shape, its color, and its vibrations. Breath in and let yourself soar to the ends of the universe; breathe out and bring the cosmos back inside. Next, breath up and all the fecundity and vibrancy of the earth. Finally, blend the breath of heaven and the breath of earth with that of your own body, becoming the breath of life itself. As you calm down, naturally let yourself settle in the heart of things. Find your center and fill yourself with light and heat.

Those who practice the art of peace must protect the domain of mother nature, the divine reflection of creation, band keep it lovely and fresh. Warriorship gives birth to natural beauty. The subtle techniques of a warrior arrive as naturally as the appearance of spring, summer, autumn, and winter. Warriorship is none other than the vitality that sustains all life.

Life is a divine gift. The divine is not something outside of us; it is right in our very center; it is our freedom. In our training, we learn the real nature of life and death. When life is victorious, there is birth; when it is thwarted, there is death. A warrior is always engaged in a life-and-death struggle for peace.

Contemplate the workings of this world, listen to the words of the wise, and take all that is good as your own. With this as your base, open your own door to truth. Do not overlook the truth that is right before you.

True wisdom comes from intellectual education, physical education, ethical education, and ki education.

Do not forget to pay your respects to the four directions each day. this wonderful world of ours is a creation of the divine, and for that gift we need to be ever grateful. That gratitude should be expressed through some kind of prayer. True prayer has no set form. Just offer your heartfelt gratitude in a way you feel is appropriate, and you will be amply rewarded.

Always keep your body filled with light and heat. Fill yourself with the power of wisdom and enlightenment.

To practice properly the art of peace, you must:

1. Calm the spirit and return to the source.
2. Cleanse the body and spirit by removing all malice, selfishness, and desire.
3. Be ever grateful for the gifts received from the universe, your relatives, mother nature, and your fellow human beings.

The art of peace is based on the four great virtues: bravery, wisdom, love, and friendship, symbolized by fire, heaven, earth, and water.

The only real sin is to be ignorant of the universal, timeless principles of existence. Such ignorance is the root of all evil and all misguided behavior. Eliminate ignorance through the art of peace, and even hell will be emptied of tortured souls.

Never fear another challenger, no matter how large; never despise another challenger, no matter how small.

Loyalty and devotion lead to bravery. Bravery leads to the spirit of self-sacrifice. The spirit of self-sacrifice creates trust in the power of love.

The purpose of training is to tighten up the slack, toughen the body, and polish the spirit.

From ancient times, deep learning and valor have been the two pillars of the path: through the virtues of training, enlighten both body and soul.

Instructors can impart a fraction of the teaching. It is through your own devoted practice that the mysteries of the art of peace are brought to life.

A true warrior is always armed with three things: the radiant sword of pacification; the mirror of bravery, wisdom, and friendship; and the precious jewel of enlightenment.

It is necessary to develop a strategy that utilizes all the physical conditions and elements that are directly at hand. The best strategy relies upon an unlimited set of responses.

The body should be triangular, the mind circular. The triangle represents the generation of energy and is most the most stable physical posture. The circle symbolizes serenity and perfection, the source of unlimited techniques. The square stands for solidity, the basis of applied control.

All of life is a circle, endlessly reviling, and that is the center point of the art of peace. The art of peace is a seamless inexhaustible sphere that encompasses all things.

Do not look upon this world with fear and loathing. Bravely face whatever the Gods offer.

Life is always a trial. In training, you must test and polish yourself in order to face the great challenges of life. Transcend the realm of life and death, and then you will be able to make your way calmly and safely through any crisis that confronts you. Attacks can come from any direction-from above, from the middle, from below; from the front, from the back; from the left, from the right. Keep centered.

The art of peace is to fulfill that which is lacking.

There are two types of ki: ordinary ki and true ki. Ordinary ki is coarse and heavy; true ki light and versatile. In order to perform well, you have to liberate yourself from ordinary ki and permeate your organs with true ki. That is the basis of powerful techniques. Ki can be a gentle breeze rustling the leaves, or a fierce wind snapping large branches.

Progress comes to those who train and train; reliance on secret techniques will get you nowhere.

Fiddling with this and that technique is of no avail. Simply act decisively without reserve!

The heart of the art of peace is: true victory is self-victory; day of swift victory! "True victory" means unflinching courage; "self-victory" symbolizes unflagging effort; and "day of swift victory" represents the glorious moment of triumph in the here and now. The art of peace is free of set forms, so it responds immediately to any contingency, which thus assures us of true victory; it is invincible because it contends with nothing. Rely on true victory, self-victory, day of swift victory and you will be able to integrate the inner and outer factors of life, clear your path of obstacles, and cleanse your senses.

Victory over oneself is the primary goal of our training. We focus on the spirit rather than the form, the kernel rather than the shell.

Cast off limiting thoughts and return to true emptiness. Stand in the midst of the great void. This is the secret of the way of war.

Ultimately you must forget about technique. The further you progress, the fewer teachings there are. The great path is really no path.

The art of peace is a form of prayer that generates light and heat. Forget about your little self, detach yourself from objects, and you will radiate light and warmth. Light is wisdom; warmth is compassion.

We can no longer rely on the external teachings of Buddha, Confucius, or Christ. The era of organized religion controlling every aspect of life is over. No single religion has all the answers.

Construction of shrine and temple buildings is not enough. Establish yourself as a living Buddha image. We all should be transformed into Goddesses of compassion or victorious Buddhas.

Holy Qur'an 92:4-7: Verily, (the ends) ye strive for are diverse. So, he who gives (in charity) and fears God, and (in all sincerity) testifies to the best-We will indeed make smooth for him the path to bliss.

Chapter7: Yoga (union)

(A) Chemistry

GOD is a theological abstraction defined by 7 characteristics:

1. Divine Simplicity (not consisting of parts)
2. Omnipresent (present everywhere, eternal)
3. Omniscient (all knowing)
4. Omnipotent (all powerful)
5. Omnibenevolent (all good)
6. Creator, Sustainer, and Destroyer
7. Giver of Life and the Bringer of Death

Based on the definition of GOD, the ELECTRON is the only Empirical object which satisfies all of the criteria as being GOD!

The ELECTRON is Divine Simplicity: The doctrine of Divine Simplicity says that GOD is without parts, not composite, and not made up of something else. The ELECTRON is a subatomic, fundamental particle, having no components or substructure.

The ELECTRON is Omnipresent: Omnipresence is the quality of being present everywhere at the same time. All Matter is composed of Atoms, and all Atoms are composed of at least 1 or more ELECTRONS. Thus, everywhere there is something, there is at least 1 ELECTRON.

The ELECTRON is Omniscient: Omniscience is the quality of knowing all information. Neurons are cells that are the core components of the Brain which process and transmit information in the form of ELECTRONS as electrical signals. ELECTRONS are what thoughts, ideas, and knowledge are made of. Literally everything that is known is facilitated by way of ELECTRONS.

The ELECTRON is Omnipotent: Omnipotence is the quality of being All Powerful. In physics, Power is the rate at which a Force does Work. All of the Forces in the Universe are based on the 4 Fundamental Forces, and ELECTRONS participate in 3 of the 4 Fundamental Forces: Gravitation, Electromagnetism, and the Electro-weak Forces. Electrons do not participate in the Strong Nuclear force, but Electrons can participate in nuclear reactions. Hence, the ELECTRON is Omnipotent.

The ELECTRON is Omnibenevolent: Omnibenevolence is the quality of being "all good", and "goodness" is defined as always adhering to a set of rules, laws, or codes. The set of rules or equations that The ELECTRON always adheres to includes the Pauli Exclusion Principle, the Schrödinger equation, the Dirac equation, Wave-Particle Duality, and Angular Momentum, just to name a few.

The ELECTRON is Creator: The exchange or sharing of ELECTRONS between two or more atoms is the main cause of chemical bonding which creates the Molecules of all substances. Conversely, the Chemical Reactions which Destroy, or transform, one substance to another involve the loss or change in position of
ELECTRONS.

The ELECTRON gives LIFE: Life is a characteristic of physical entities having Biological processes, and Biological processes are any number of Chemical Reactions that results in a transformation. Chemical Reactions are caused by the loss or change in position of ELECTRONS. Conversely, the cessation of Chemical Reactions, is when ELECTRONS stop flowing, and is what brings about Death.

Some additional similarities between GOD and the ELECTRON are:

- Love: It is said by people in various religions that "GOD is Love". As a thought or emotion, the feeling of Love occurs due to the movement of ELECTRONS in the brain and body.

- Light: It is said by people in various religions that GOD created Light by saying "Let there be Light". ELECTRONS moving from higher Orbital Shells to lower Orbital Shells is the origin of Light.

- In the Clouds: It is said by people in various religions that "GOD is in the Clouds". ELECTRONS orbit the nucleus of an atom in ELECTRON CLOUDS.

- You Can't See God or ELECTRONS: It is said by people in various religions that "you cannot see GOD". Currently there is no method in existence to directly see an ELECTRON or any subatomic particle.

Electrons in the Atomic Model: Atoms and Electrons have never been directly seen, but scientists have proved that sub-atomic particles exist through experimentation which facilitates a consistent method to observe the effects made through predictions provided by the Atomic Model. A model is a representation of a system in the real world and is intended to help us understand systems and their properties. The atomic model represents what the structure of an atom could look like, based on what we know about how atoms behave. It is not necessarily a true picture of the exact structure of an atom. Models are often simplified and cannot always be absolutely accurate.

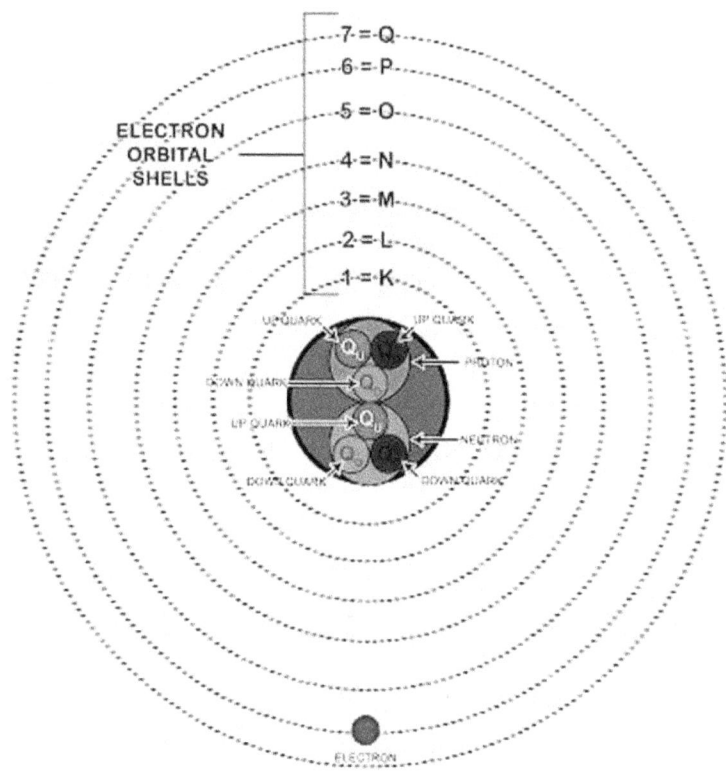

PTAH as an Ancient African ELECTRON "Model":

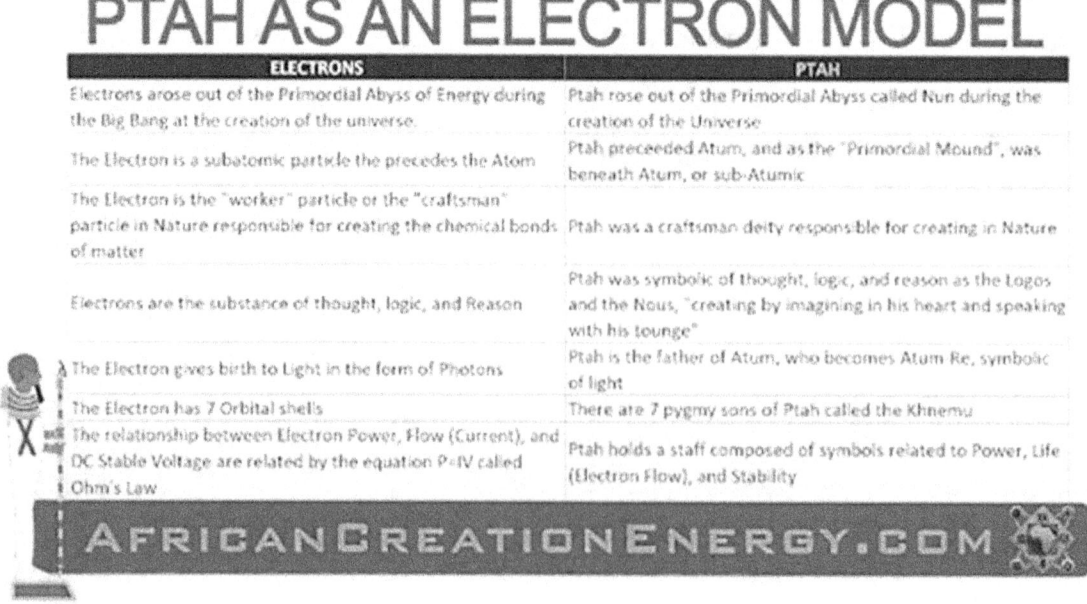

Relationship Between EL and PTAH: "The Egyptian god Ptah is given the title ḏū gitti 'Lord of Gath' in a prism from Lachish which has on its opposite face the name of Amenhotep II (c. 1435–1420

BCE) The title ḏū gitti is also found in Serābiṭṭ text 353. Cross (1973, p. 19) points out that Ptah is often called the Lord (or one) of eternity and thinks it may be this identification of 'Ēl with Ptah that lead to the epithet 'olam 'eternal' being applied to 'Ēl so early and so consistently." SOURCE: Cross, Frank Moore (1973). Canaanite Myth and Hebrew Epic. Cambridge, MA: Harvard University Press. ISBN 978-0-674-09176-4.

EL is the Origin of the Name of God in Judeo-Christian, Islamic, and various Mesopotamian Religions:

אֵל	EL (Strong's H410)	God (Hebrew)
אֱלוֹהַּ	Eloh (Strong's H433)	God (Hebrew)
אֱלֹהִים	Elohiym (Strong's H430)	Gods (Hebrew)
الله	Allah (Islamic Quran)	God (Arabic)
𒀭	ilu	God (Akkadian)

EL (the origin of the Mesopotamian name for God) is in the word ELECTRON:
- **EL** - "Mesopotamian word for God"
- **LECT** - "word, speech, thought" (Greek lexis and logos)
- **TRON** - Greek suffix referring to a device, tool, or instrument

(B) The Resurrection

THE OTHER MEANING OF CHRISTMAS

By Judith and Riley Hansard Crabb

The literal minded person believes that Jesus was born just about the way it is described in the Christmas story and this satisfies him. The questioning, thinking person may very well wonder if there isn't any deeper significance hidden behind or within the veil of words. There is good reason to suspect this because it is said the Disciples received special information in the Upper Room while the multitudes were taught in parables.

The purpose of all so-called sacred writings is to convey a higher or deeper meaning than the literal story used by the teacher.

Commonplace words and events must be used to attract the attention, but they can also convey esoteric ideas which can be grasped only by the awakened understanding of a student of metaphysics. "Let thine eye be single", say the Scriptures; however, if a Spiritual or psychological opening of that "eye" has not taken place, the reader of the Gospel stories will only see their literal meaning. Nevertheless, if the higher meaning we speak of is to be understood, ordinary words and knowledge <u>must</u> be used as a starting point.

The object of the parables given by Jesus was to instruct thinking men and women in the higher or sacred wisdom. A parable has a meaning beyond its literal sense; it is designed to work toward lifting the mind above the ordinary level to something higher. It might be said that it transforms thought.

We can take an example from the Ten Commandments. The 7th one says, "Thou shalt not commit adultery". The literal meaning of this is obvious enough but the psychological or spiritual meaning is quite something else to the awakened mind. It warns the student not to adulterate one set of doctrine or teachings with those of another School.

Let us take another Commandment, "Thou shalt not steal". The literal meaning of this is obvious but what of the psychological or Spiritual meaning? To the student it contains the admonition not to delude himself with his own self-importance. This 8th Commandment refers to an attitude of blind independence all too common to mankind. The rugged individualist, the man of the world, thinks that he does everything from himself, by his own power, giving no credit to God, this is stealing in a psychological sense. It is doubtful if the ordinary man would understand this if it were told to him directly. He would think it ridiculous or turn the meaning to suit his own ends. This is why sacred teachings must be concealed by an outer wrapping. [2] There is no deliberate intention by Jesus and other advanced teachers to mislead people.

They just want to make sure their teaching doesn't fall in the wrong place.

INNER EVOLUTION STARTS WITH CHRISTMAS

The development of understanding is a long slow process and it must come from within. This the central idea of the Gospels. They are concerned mainly with this inner evolution which begins with the Christmas story. This is the significance of the literal story of the birth of the infant Jesus. Its higher meaning is the constant rebirth of Higher Consciousness in every person by degrees.

Man is a seed capable of infinite growth. This is what the Gospel stories are concerned with. The outer side of our lives is pretty well organized according to our position and capacity. It is the inner side which can be awakened, stimulated and developed by contact with the Higher meaning of the Sacred Scriptures. They give us an idea, an understanding of what we must do, feel, and think to forward our most important <u>inner</u> evolution. Now, with a single eye, let us consider the Christmas Story in greater detail.

It symbolizes an <u>initiation</u>. The Nativity of the Christ represents the beginning of a new cycle. The new cycle could be the beginning of a universe, the beginning of a Solar system, the beginning of a new civilization, birth into the physical world for a human being or, of prime interest to us right now, the dawn of a Spiritual awakening in the human heart. Christmas really is the festival of a Spiritual birth. True, it happened 2000 years ago to Jesus, but somewhere in the world it happens every day to men and women. There is a Christmas of the soul.

The Gospel story, historically accurate or not, reveals the final Way of Holiness which lies before every man and woman. To the religious or mystic type, the goal is sainthood. To the intellectual or hermetic type, the goal is adeptship; so, the Gospel story is a mighty parable. Jesus himself explains it in Luke 8:4-15:

"4, And when a great multitude came together; and they of every city resorted unto him, he spake by a parable: 5, The sower went forth to sow his seeds and as he sowed, some fell by the way side; and it was trodden under foot, and the birds of the heaven devoured it. 6, And other fell on the rock; and as soon as it grew, it withered away, because it had no moisture. 7, And other fell amidst the thorns; and the thorns grew with it and choked it. 8, And other fell into the good ground, and grew, and brought forth fruit a hundredfold. As he said these things, he cried, He that hath ears to hear, let him hear.

"9, And his disciples asked him what this parable might be. 10, And he said, unto you it is given to know the mysteries of the kingdom of God; but to the rest in parables; that seeing they may not see and hearing they may not understand. 11, Now the parable is this: The seed is the word of God. 12, And those by the way side are they that have heard; then cometh the devil, and taketh away the Word from their heart, that they may not believe and be saved. 13, And those on the rock are they who, when they have heard, receive the word with joy; and these have no root, who for a while believe, I and in time of temptation fall away. 14, And that which fell among the thorns, these are they that heard, and as they go on their way they are choked with cares and riches and pleasures of this life and bring no fruit to perfection. 15, And that in the good ground, these are such as in an honest and good heart, having heard the word, hold it fast, and bring forth fruit with patience."

IN THE WORLD BUT ON THE PATH

Once the true purpose of the Gospel stories is understood the thinking person realizes it is ridiculous to insist on the literal interpretation of the birth of Jesus, or to claim that it is historically accurate. The Spiritual leaders of the time altered history to suit the needs of the Spiritual truths they wished to impart.

To the student of metaphysics Christmas is more important as a symbol of awakening self-consciousness. For him the Nativity means the opening up of intuitive vision. Naturally, this brings knowledge of the Oneness of life.

The result of this is or should be that he gives himself to service to the Light. Those who have responded to this Light, or to the call of the Spirit if you will, are determined to mold their life according to the Principles enunciated by the Savior.

They may still be in the world but are on the Path. The Christ is the Spiritual exemplar for all in the Western World regardless of whether they look up to Him or not. But those who are awakened and determined to change find themselves living the Gospel story as an interior experience even if they do not go through the actual physical incidents as Jesus did.

The awakened person who studies deeply the Gospel Story is going to become aware of initiations as definite steps or milestones on the Path. The word "initiation" is derived from the Latin "initia". This simply means First Principles. Initiation into a Special group or order is an idea as ancient as mankind. For thousands of years the term initiate has been applied specifically to a person who has had revealed to him the Secrets of occult science. This Ancient Wisdom is taught in Mystery Schools. The Greek name for such teachers is Hierophant, [4] literally this means "one who explains things" but the name was generally given to the chief initiate of a Mystery School.

In modern times, unawakened people are likely to believe that Mystery Schools, initiates and ceremonial magic are all things of the ancient past; but the awakened know that the Mystery Teachings are alive today; and that initiations are still being given to the worthy in the Lodges.

THE CHRISTMAS INITIATION

The Christmas initiation then is the birth of Christ consciousness in the heart. This is the first of the Great Initiations, so-called. There are five which lead to complete mastery of the flesh and therefore freedom from the wheel of re-birth. The other four initiations in order of their taking are: Baptism (Matthew 3:13), Transfiguration (Matthew 17:2), Crucifixion (Matthew 27-35), and

Ascension (The Acts 1-9) to the stature of the fullness of the Christ. So, the student of metaphysics must realize that the Christmas story and the Gospels have two meanings:

1. The passage of Jesus through these initiations.

2. The indication of the five great steps or stages along the Path which lie ahead of every sincere student and man of good will.

The Four Gospels then are really a skillful blend of history and fiction designed to instruct and inspire those who seek Truth in the Western World. As the Teacher says in John 18:37 "every one that is of the Truth, heareth my voice."

The sequence of these five initiations is a natural growth-cycle in life and repeated in lesser degree in every one's life in many different growth situations. These are rehearsals for the Great Initiations by which every human being eventually winds up his human existence. As Geoffrey Hodson says, "We all have nativity, conversion, baptism of sorrow, transfiguration or upliftment, betrayals and crucifixions, and our recoveries and ascensions."

All of these elements are woven together in the Gospel stories. There is the story of life of Jesus as a man entering on the Path of Initiation and moving on to adepthood through the five Great Initiations; but this is also occult instruction to the awakened man. In the Gospels he is given information on natural law which he can apply to the universe, to the solar system, to the human race and to individuals like himself.

As man experiences this five-fold cycle over and over and [5] over again in many lives his Soul grows. Through the material losses and the spiritual gains from all of the outside influences upon him, he experiences natural evolution; but he need not wait for the mass of mankind as it moves painfully slowly along the circular path of return to the Father's house.

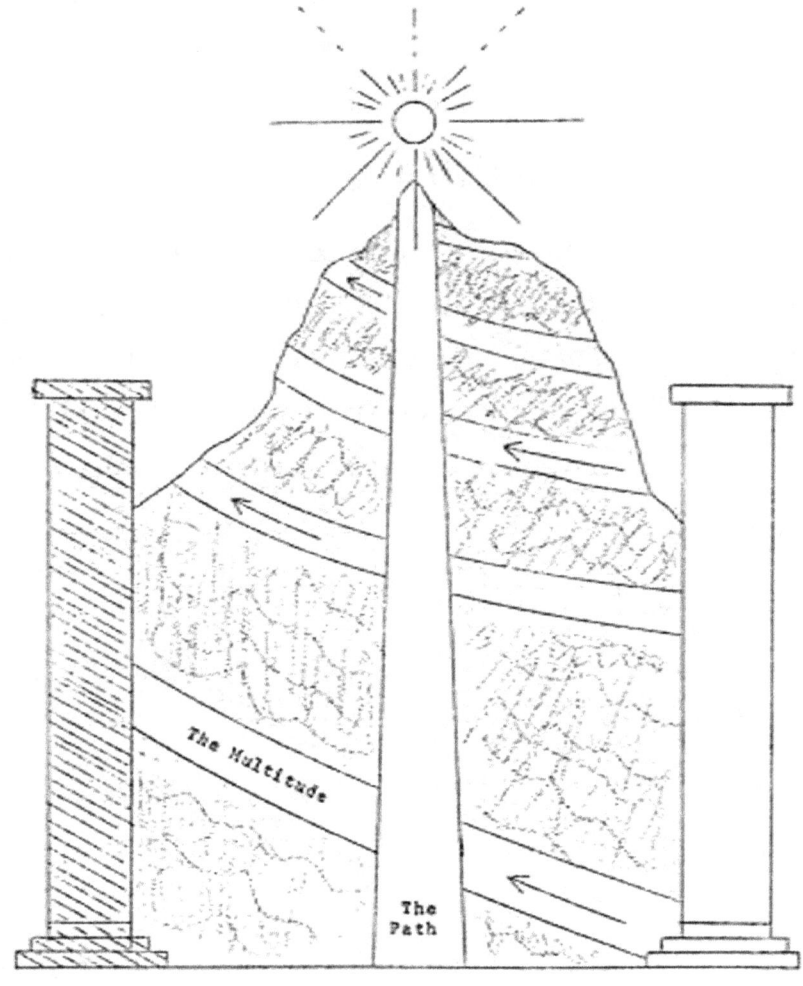

"Straight is the Gate, Narrow is the Way"

THE TRUE ANNUNCIATION

Once an individual has developed enough intelligence to glimpse the goal of evolution and to understand it, he can undertake the self-quickening process, as distinct from natural evolution. It is the quickening power of his own Divine Self, the I AM, which stirs the Divine discontent within him. This is the true Annunciation. It is also the Voice of conscience. The symbol of that from the Christ story is John the Baptist. The call issued by Jesus in the Gospel story is to awaken men and women to enter the narrow path, through the straight gate.

The Christmas story, then, is a call to enter upon the Way. This happens when Christ is born, in the Mystical sense, in the heart center, Tiphareth on the Tree of Life. This includes the solar plexus. Let us see how the story of the Nativity describes His birth as an interior experience. Here are the four clues by which you read the Christmas story with the eye of the Spirit. "Let thine eye be single."

1. The story happens within;

2. It dramatizes the soul's experience;

3. The historical people in the Nativity are personifications of principles, or the lack of them, in man;

4. All objects in the story have symbolical meaning.

If the Gospel story is an interior experience and people are personifications of principles, what of John the Baptist?

He is the voice of the Higher Self manifesting in the personality as conscience. The voice of our conscience is the call from on high reminding us of the Continual choices between right and wrong in any given situation. In the Old Testament this same idea is portrayed by one of the prophets when he shouts from his wilderness retreat, "Repent ye for the Kingdom of Heaven is at hand." This is just another way or reminding a student that Divinity is within him always, exerting a subtle but steady pressure toward self-improvement.

THE ANGEL OF THE ANNUNCIATION

In the Christmas story the Voice of the High Self is symbolized by the Angels who appeared to the Shepherds and <u>announced</u> the coming birth. Remember, this describes the inner experience of the descent of the Holy Power from a world of eternal Light into the heart and solar plexus of the personality. This Birth is a profound psychological awakening, a development of new power from within the soul. There is a physiological awakening in the body to accompany the psychological awakening. This is the Immaculate Conception.

THE PHYSIOLOGICAL AWAKENING

Dr. George W. Carey tells us what happens in the physical body when the Immaculate Conception takes place. On either side of the thalamus in the head is a gland. The one in back is the pineal; the one in front is the pituitary. The pineal is cone-shaped and secretes a yellow fluid. The pituitary body opposite it is ellipsoid in shape and contains a whitish secretion, like milk.

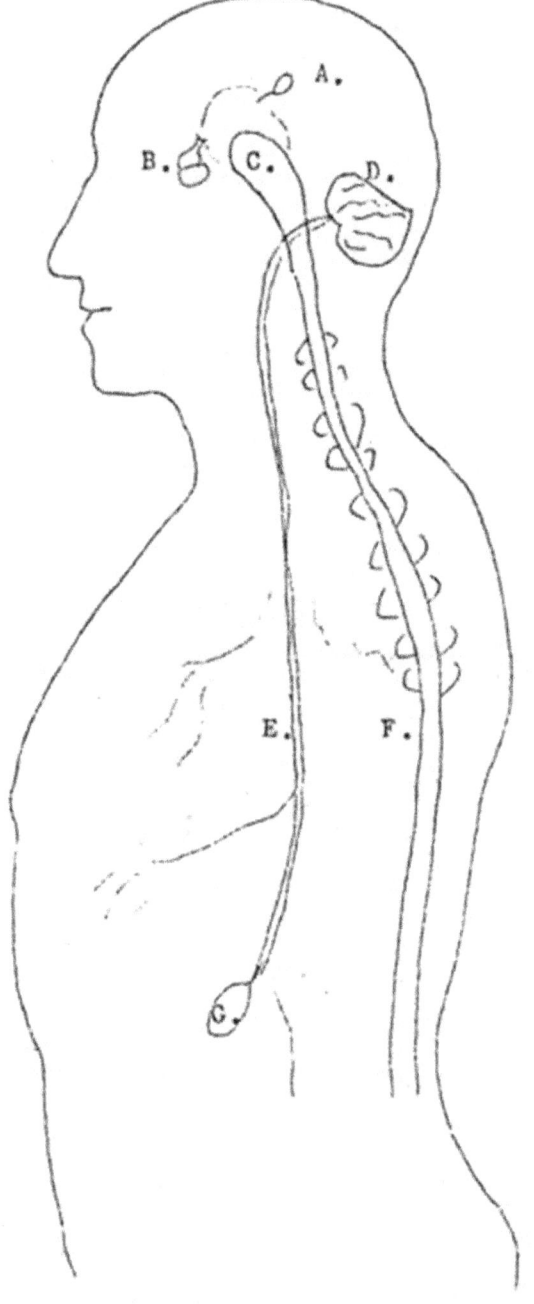

A. Pineal Gland (Joseph)
B. Pituitary Body (Mary)
C. Medulla Oblongata
D. Cerebellum
E. Pneumogastric Nerve
F. Spinal Column
G. Solar Plexus
   (Cave of the Nativity)

    The fluids that are found in both of these bodies came from the same source, the claustrum, which means barrier or cloister. It is referred to as a cloister for the very good reason that a precious and holy thing is secreted there. <u>Saint</u> <u>Claus</u> or Santa Claus is another term for this precious fluid, which indeed is a holy gift in the body of each one of us.

ELECTRIC SUN AND MAGNETIC MOON

The precious fluid which flees down from the claustrum separates, part going into the pineal gland and part to the pituitary body. These, being special laboratories in the head, differentiate the fluid from the claustrum and it takes on the colors above mentioned. In the pineal gland it becomes yellow and has electric properties. The milk-like fluid in the pituitary has magnetic properties.

These two glands are male and female, the Joseph and Mary of the physical body. They are the parents of the Spiritual Son born in the solar plexus of each human being commencing at about the age of 12. The yellow and white material is the milk and honey referred to in the Bible. The Children of Israel were given the promise of a return to this land flowing with milk and honey. The yellow and white fluids reach the solar plexus via the semi-lunar ganglia (pneumogastric nerve). The plexus is the Bethlehem of the physical body. In Hebrew, Bethlehem means House (both) of Bread (lehem). "I am the bread of life", said the allegorical Jesus (seed).

In the solar plexus is a thimble-shaped depression, a cave or manger: and in this is deposited the psycho-physical seed, or holy child, born of this Immaculate Conception. This psycho-physical seed is also called the fish; as it has the odor of fish and is formed in the midst of the waters, the pure water. St. Augustine wrote: "Jesus is a fish in the midst of the waters."

Before birth the human fetus floats like a fish in the fluids by which it is surrounded. And as it is with the child formed on the generative plane, so it is with the Spiritual child born in the solar plexus, Bethlehem. Joseph and Mary, by furnishing the material for the Spiritual child, which was to redeem the child or body-form in generation, paid the symbolical redemption money. The breath, descending the pneumo-gastric nerve into the solar center, enter the manger where Joseph and Mary are, and where Jesus the seed is "literally conceived by the Holy Ghost".

OCCULT OBSERVATION BY AUGUSTA FOSS HEINDEL

"Let us observe a subject, a woman in Spiritual meditation, one who has been living a pure and chaste life with high aspirations, and whose food for years has consisted of [9] fruit, vegetables and cereals. The pituitary body, through which these aspirations are first registered, is much enlarged. The posterior lobe is turned backward with its funnel shaped neck enlarged with a mouth opening at the end. From this open mouth exudes gas of a soft rose color, slightly intermingled with yellow and blue of pale shades.

"The Spinal column is filled with a pale blue ether, intermingled with soft pink and yellow. After this gas leaves the medulla oblongata and enters the pineal gland, it is of a wonderful blue color such as one seas clinging to the mountains after sundown. The pineal gland is enlarged with the point of the cone leaning forward toward the pituitary body. The tiny appendage of skin at the end of the former . . . is elongated and emits a small flame similar to the blue flame of a gas jet. These two organs vibrate at a most rapid rate and lean toward each other over the third ventricle. This Ventricle is an oblong cavity lying between the optic thalami. When the life of the aspirant has been pure, the ventricle appears to the occultist like a tiny furnace with a golden glow.

"The pineal gland, as already stated, has the appearance of a tiny male organ, while the pituitary body with its open mouth is similar to the female organ. So, we may see that science, which is trying to prove that these organs are directly connected with the functions of the brain and the generative organs, is right. They have direct influence upon man from the two ends of the spinal cord, for does not the sex pervert in time become a degenerate? Conservation of the vital fluids and a chaste life strengthen the brain, and these two ductless glands become enlarged, but in the sensualist, they atrophy . . ."

FATHER, SON, AND HOLY GHOST

Occult science teaches that a personality is made up of a lower trinity of physical body, emotions and mind. Even the man of the world will admit to these three. The awakened man, on the other hand, becomes aware of his triple soul or higher bodies. It is the latent power of these that begin to come into play when Christ is born in the human heart-solar plexus.

Traditionally, the Archangel Gabriel is supposed to have announced to Mary that she was most fortunate of Women. But in this interior experience of which we speak, Gabriel represents or is the messenger of the High Self, the I Am, in lighting the Divine flame in the heart.

What does Mary symbolize as the personification of a Divine Principle? She represents the soul, the Higher Self. The infant Jesus represents love and intuition. Intuition gives a person the power to apprehend truth directly; so, he cannot be deceived. Love guides him to an intelligent use of his new Power and Wisdom. Joseph represents the illumined concrete mind in the Christmas story. Because this is an [10] immaculate conception, between the Higher Self and the Lower Self or personality and not between man and Woman, Joseph is the foster-father of intuition.

ANIMALS AND CREEPING THINGS

Another interesting symbol in the manger scene in the Christmas story is the animals. Some artists depict only domestic animals as one would expect to find in the stable of an inn: horses and cows, dogs and cats. But artists whose inspiration comes from a deeper source will include reptiles and creeping things. These represent the elemental forces of the interior of the earth, uncivilized, untamed. The domestic animals represent purified emotions, under civilized control.

The manger itself is a symbol of nourishment, a source of life. In the whole man this is the heart-solar plexus, also the etheric double. The next larger structure in this Christmas picture is the stable. This is the physical body. The inn nearby or outside the stable is the outside world with all of its cross currents, confusion and normal worldly life.

THE HIGHER TRINITY

In the Western Mystery Tradition, the three-fold powers of the Cosmic Man, the Highest Self or I Am, are termed Power, Wisdom and Love. Sometimes these three are referred to as Omnipotence, Omniscience and Omnipresence.

The Angels represent Omnipotence, the Divine Will which descends into Mary, the Higher Self as an act of creation. This is the immaculate conception on a higher level. When this Spiritual Will is developed in a person he has Omnipotence. As we said, Joseph represents the concrete mind of the personality. He cannot "father" the child to be because Spiritual qualities cannot be generated by the intellect. Intelligence is a combination of knowledge and experience wisely directed by the soul. When this higher mental power, abstract mind or intuition, is developed it gives a person Omniscience.

Love, or Omnipresence, is the result of the union of the previous two. Spiritual power, Mary, fructifies the lower mind and the result is the birth of Divine perception and the realization of the Oneness of all life. Omnipresence is universal love.

Everyone knows that virgin birth is ridiculous or impossible under normal circumstances. What else can the writers of the Christmas story intend than to shock the reader? They want the searching person to realize that this is not a historical event but an allegory! This is the story of the interior Spiritual awakening. The story itself is a blind which turns [11] the worldly person away from a Great Mystery for which he is not yet ready. For the union of Power and Wisdom within the awakening man or woman is indeed an Immaculate Conception. The product of that union is Divine Love.

A CLOSER LOOK AT THE STABLE

Why must this virgin birth take place in a stable? And why should this manifestation from on high come as an infant? Here is a hint of the greatest Spiritual Truth for mankind in the flesh. "Life is fulfilled by renunciation." This golden thread runs through the whole of the Gospel story.

The renunciation of worldly possessions, power and privilege are symbolized in this humble birth amid poverty. Jesus attained his kingship by renouncing the world. This idea was born out later when he matured and entered his ministry. He was despised and rejected of men.

This is a course of behavior which one hesitates to offer to the public; for it is the opposite of the principles which move most men to action. The story of the Nativity offers a code of ethics so high that it can be spoken of only with an apology. It poses a problem in behavior beyond all the bounds of logic. Does the renewal of life depend upon death? So, it seems; for He said, "He that loseth his life for my sake shall gain it unto life eternal."

What is there to be renounced if we would receive the Kingdom of Heaven? It is really a state of mind, a personal attitude toward personal possessions, higher position, the love and esteem of our friends. If there is to be a birth of Christ Light in our hearts there must be detachment, disinterestedness. This is the preparation for the Nativity. Remember, it is more an interior change of attitude than an exterior getting rid of worldly possessions. If a person has worldly responsibilities he must have the means to fulfill these responsibilities.

The difference is between possessions for their own sake or for the means to get the essential work done. On the other hand, too many religious fanatics have taken the preparation for the Nativity too literally and have thrown common sense and wisdom to the winds -- along with worldly goods which were necessary to carry on the Great Work. If power and possessions are held, they are for service. If friendship is given, it is without possessiveness, and the same is true of love.

WANT NOTHING AND HAVE EVERYTHING

In the highest sense, that which is renounced is retained forevermore once the spirit of hoarding is outgrown. He who wants for nothing has everything, obviously; for it was during the renunciation in the manger that the kings and the Magi came to lay their worldly treasures at the feet of the Babe.

This philosophical concept is beyond the understanding of the worldly man or woman, who anyhow would despise the stable of an inn as a resting place; but only here could a Mystic Birth occur; for the would-be initiate must be <u>rejected</u> by worldly men if he is to be <u>accepted</u> by Spiritual men!

There is an august assembly of Adepts on the inner planes at the birth of Christ. They represent a power which the disciple covets but which appears as nothing in the eyes of men. For the gentleness which is demanded of a student on the Path is despised as weakness in the world outside. The great Chinese Sage, Lao Tse, said, "When Heaven would preserve a man it enfolds him in gentleness."

THE STAR OF BETHLEHEM

One important symbol in the Manger scene is the star which shines forth at the time. This is a symbol of initiation. It indicates the increase of Spiritual power in the initiates. It is also a symbol of the one Initiator for the race of mankind on this earth; for it is by His power that all initiations are conferred. It is when His Spiritual rod of power touches the soul of the student on the Path that the Christ-child is born in the Bethlehem of the heart-solar plexus center.

Now in 1967 we are in a great world-wide crisis at the end of this Piscean Age. The Rod of Initiation is touching mankind as a whole. A <u>racial</u> Nativity is taking place. The Spirit of Brotherhood, a larger, more impersonal love is being born in the hearts of those humans ready to receive it.

In this world-wide conflict the resistance of conservatives to change and the crystallization of old and honored Piscean institutions are represented in the Christmas story by Herod. This Hebrew King represents materialism, selfishness, self-indulgence and pride. He truly recognizes that the New Light of the New Age dawning threatens the end of all that he considers important; so, he must attack and destroy.

In the Christmas story, Joseph, Mary and the Babe flee to Egypt, the home of the Western Mystery Tradition. This represents, symbolically, the place of Light, a land where there is progress.

THE LAST OF THE HEBREW PROPHETS

The voice crying in the wilderness, the voice of John the Baptist, is symbolically the Higher Self calling to the Lower, trying to awaken the worldly man to his own Divinity. The voice in the wilderness is also the conscience calling to the Lower Self to renounce its Worldly ways, to repent over-indulgence and willful wrong doing. Thus, the Higher Self constantly pleads with the Lower to purify itself in the quest for perfection. Here again, in the Gospel story, the [13] historical figure of the Baptist symbolizes an interior experience. The voice crying in the wilderness is an insistent demand to which every man and woman must respond someday.

In relation to the Christ idea, John represents that soul about to enter upon the Path. On the larger scene of the human race today, John the Baptist represents the highly civilized men of East or West who are pushing the idea of brotherhood through the United Nations. But before the ideal of world-wide peace through cooperation can be achieved individual nations must give up their desire for power and possessions. To come back to the individual man represented by John, he must be free from personal desire.

SALOME AND WHY SHE DANCED

In the Gospel story the selfish human passions are represented by the dancer, Salome. You remember what happened, John rejected her seductive advances, his head was out off, and the lower man died to the higher.

John's refusal to give way to the passions represented by Salome symbolizes the austerities to which the student must subject himself. He must bring his animal passions under control and free himself from the skeptical, critical, limiting concrete mind. The beheading symbolizes the soul's freedom from the lower mind!

We could say that Salome represents the personal or Lower Self and John represents the soul or Higher Self, in this story. Her personal ambitions danced upon the passions and aroused desire and arrogance. This in turn created Spiritual blindness and cruelty. But the very act of demanding John's head is an act of grace; for this "death" is really a victory over the defeated Lower Self. To take the symbology further, the prison is John's body and beheading frees him from it. To consciously rise above limitations, desire must be transmuted into Will. The lower mind must be slain before this can happen. The lower mind foretells or prophesies the coming of the Higher and dies when the Higher is born. Thus, did John the Baptist foretell the coming of the Christ. John's life ended when Christ began His mission. Thus, does the lower die to the Higher.

THREE SIGNS OF THE FIRST GREAT INITIATION

This is the interior experience of the soul as it prepares for the first of the Great Initiations, the birth of the Babe in the heart. There are three signs that precede it:

1. The prophecy of the coming Messiah.
2. The Annunciation.
3. The ministry of John the Baptist.

These three really tell of the awakening of the conscience and of the increasing pressure of the Higher Self on the personality toward repentance and a definite change in the way of life.

THE CONTINUAL RE-WRITING OF THE ANCIENT WISDOM

In recounting the allegories of the Gospel story, we must keep in mind that the sacred literature of every race is written by men and women who know the Ancient Wisdom. Civilizations and nations must come and go but the Lodges of the Masters on the Inner Planes, and the Sages and Saints who compose their memberships, endure from age to age. It is their duty to preserve the Divine or Ancient Wisdom and to re-issue it through new channels -- Students, initiates and Adapts in the flesh -- as man and nation are ready to receive it.

Every generation of mankind requires a re-writing of the Mysteries if the Ancient Wisdom is to appeal to the modern minds of the day. The followers of an Adept teacher tend to turn his liberal ideas into conservative dogma. Priesthoods then combine the material into an organized religion. Like all man-made institutions, organized religions outlive their usefulness and must come to an end. There is an ensuing dark age and then nations rise again. Again, Adept teachers come to enunciate a portion of the Ancient Wisdom, partially revealed but again partially concealed from the eyes of the profane.

Galatians 4:21-26: (21) Tell me, ye that desire to be under the law, do ye not hear the law? (22) For it is written, that Abraham had two sons, the one by a bondmaid, the other by a free woman. (23) But he who was of the bondwoman was born after the flesh; but he of the free woman was by promise. (24) Which things are an **allegory**: for these two are covenants; the one from mount Si'nai, which gendereth to bondage, which is Hagar. (25) For Hagar is mount Si'nai in Arabia, and answereth to Jerusalem which now is in bondage with her children. (26) But Jerusalem which is above is free, which is the mother of us all.

Luke 8:17-18:(17)For nothing is secret, that shall not be made manifest; neither anything hid, that shall not be known and come abroad.(18)Take heed therefore how ye hear; for whosoever hath, to him shall be given; and whosoever hath not, from him shall be taken even that which he seemeth to have.

(C) Completing the circle/*circuit*:

One who is unattached to the fruits of his work and who works as he is obligated is in the renounced order of life, and he is the true mystic; not he who lights no fire and performs no work.

In every one's life there are two duties: one is to serve the illusion, and the other is to serve the reality. One has to innerstand/overstand, however, that he is in all circumstances forced to serve. Either he serves the illusion or the reality. The constitutional position of the living being is to be a servant, not a master. One may think that he is the master, but he is actually a servant. One may think that he is the master of his wife, or his children or his home, business and so on, but that is all false. One is actually the servant of his wife, of his children and of his business. Our position is always as servant-either as servants of the illusion or as servant of the Creator. Of course, everyone is thinking that he is not a servant, that he is working only for himself. Although the fruits of his labor are transient and illusory, they force him to become a servant of illusion or a servant of his own senses. But when one awakens to his transcendental senses and actually becomes situated in knowledge, he then becomes a servant of the reality. When one comes to the platform of knowledge, he: innerstands/overstands that in all circumstances he is a servant. Since it is not possible for him to be master, he is much better situated serving the reality instead of the illusion. When one becomes aware of this, he has attained the platform of real knowledge. This is a matter of realization not social status.

When one has molded his life in such a way-dovetailing his desires to love and innerstanding-then it is to be known that he has attained perfection in harmony/union. Simply breathing deeply and doing some exercises is not yoga (union). A whole purification is required.

Beings should have their minds trained in such a way that as soon as their mind wanders from meditation on love, he drags it back again. This requires a great deal of practice. One must come to know that his real happiness is in experiencing the pleasure of transcendental senses, not the material senses. Senses are not to be sacrificed, and desires are not to be sacrificed, but there are both desires and sense gratification in the spiritual sphere. Real happiness transcends material, sensual experiences. If one is not convinced of this, he will surely be agitated and fall down. One should know that the happiness he desires from material senses is not really happiness.

A being is said to be established in self-realization and is called enlightened when they are fully satisfied by virtue of acquired knowledge and realization. Such a being is situated in elevation/ascension and is self-controlled. He sees everything-whether it be pebbles, stones of gold-as the same.

Theoretical knowledge alone will not help. One has to be able to apply this knowledge. Simply comprehending 'I am not this body' and at the same time acting in a nonsensical way will not help. There are many societies where the members seriously discuss practical philosophy while smoking, drinking and leading a sensual life. Knowledge must be demonstrated. One who truly innerstands 'I am not the body' will actually reduce his bodily necessities to a minimum. When one increases the demands of the body while thinking 'I am not the body', then of what use is that knowledge? A being can only be satisfied when there is theoretical knowledge and practical knowledge side by side.

When a being is situated on a practical level of spiritual realization, it should be innerstood he is actually situated in unity/harmony.

And what is the sign of practical realization? The mind will be calm and quiet and no longer agitated by the attraction of the material world. Thus self-controlled, one is not attracted by the material glitter, and sees everything-silver, dirt or diamonds-as the same.

A man must elevate self by their own mind, not degrade themselves. The mind is the friend of the conditioned soul, and his enemy as well. We have to raise ourselves to the spiritual standard by ourselves. In this sense I am my only friend and I am my only enemy. The opportunity is ours.

(D) Heart, soul, and science:

- The heart is our most powerful organ: there is no subtleness about the immense physical power of the heart. The brain's power pales by comparison. The heart is the largest generator of electromagnetic energy in our body and produces, sends, and receives a **broad** spectrum of other types and frequencies of energy occurring over time.

- The heart responds directly to the environment: it can be demonstrated that the heart reacts to electromagnetic energy outside the body. It contracts when an electromagnet is placed near it. The heart also reacts neuro-hormonally to the outside world not only in response to the brain but sometimes without the brain's awareness.

- The heart is a conductor of the energy of the body's cells: the energy from the heart, while strong, does not have to be strong to influence cellular functioning. The subtle form of energy emitted, conducted, and received by the heart is sufficient to cause significant changes in the cells of the body that may be described as info-energetic cellular memories.

- The heart is a dynamic system: the heart, like all living systems, is an open, fluctuating, interacting system. As quantum physics teaches about all systems, it expresses itself as energy, matter, and information, and it is as much waves of energy as particles of matter.

- The heart is the body's primary organizing force: the heart holds us together. It is the maker of the gestalt that we call "me" and the catalyst for mind that is our experience of "us". It uses its info energy to connect our brain and body and works in coordination with the brain but is not directed by it. Unless we remain numb to the code of the heart, neglect it, and leave the lethal covenant between a selfish, survivalist brain and hyper-responsive body unchallenged, the heart can serve its natural role as the major organizer, integrator, and balancer of the body's vital energy and can play a unique and major role in the coordinating of our cell's memories of what it means to be healthy.

- The heart resonates with information-containing energy: energy, matter, and information are one and the same. Wherever any of these three characteristics of nature is present, the other two are also "there" in some form whether we see them or not. Whenever we send or receive energy, we also are communicating information. When the heart beats out its energy, it sends information and affects the "matter" within us and outside of us. Energy going into matter is the information that becomes memory. No matter how subtle and as yet immeasurable, memory exists within matter in the form of energy, and the heart may be able to communicate that memory.

- The heart is the body system's core: because of the heart's central location in our body and the extensive connection it has to all the cells within our body, its energy transmission becomes highly influential for our body and all of the bodies around us. The heart is constantly pumping energy and information to, from, and within every cell in our body.

- The heart "speaks" and sends information: we can learn to decipher the heart's code by silencing the brain, quieting ourselves, focusing on our heart, and sensing what it has to say and what memories it may bring forth from the cells that store it. The heart has its own form of wisdom, different from that of the rational brain but every bit as important to our living, loving, working, and healing.

- All hearts exchange info with other hearts and brains: cardiac energy patterns have dynamic interactive effects. When one heart sends energy to another, that energy becomes a part of the receiving heart's memory. When the receiving heart becomes a sending heart, the energy it sends is no longer just its own. It blends its energy with the memory of the vibrations of the energy it has received. This resonating process continues infinitely, meaning that with every beat of our heart, we continue to create the info energetic vibrations that become our collective soul.

Taoism: "Man consisting of triune of spirit, mind and body, cometh forth from the eternal, and after putting off desire re-enters the glory of Tao."

Brahmanism: "Man's inner self is one with the self of the universe, and to that universe and to that unity it must return."

Buddhism: "Man, fundamentally divine, is held in the three worlds by desire. Purification from desire leads the man to nirvana."

Hebraism: "Man came into being through emanation from the will of the king, therefore is divine."

Egyptian: : Teaches the divinity of man, Osiris as his source."

Zoroastrianism: "Man is a spark of the universal flame to be ultimately united with its source."

Orphic: "Man has in him potentially the sum and substance of the universe."

Christian: Man made in the image of God- body, soul and spirit- a trinity."

- The man who knows not, but knows not that he knows not, is a fool; shun him.
- The man who knows not and knows that he knows not is a student, teach him.
- The man who knows, but knows not that he knows, is asleep; awaken him.
- The man who knows and knows that he knows is a teacher; learn from him.

"Read not to contradict and confute; nor to believe and take for granted; nor to find talk and discourse, but to weigh and consider." --Sir Francis Bacon.

Outro

Asalaamu Alaikum to all who bliss this manuscript with your energy. I am grateful for your consciousness and it is my intent to that this book has expanded your awareness and filled you with divine inspiration. Naturally, I have observed through my short life the power of positive thought and the asset of right information for the benefit of accurate knowledge, wisdom and innerstanding. Change is constant, but it doesn't appear to bold to those who choose to look through a dirty looking glass. We as sentient beings are gifted with a natural intuitive awareness and if we but listen we quickly can find what it is we search for which is ultimately peace of mind. Because we choose the life we live and the means by which we are sustained, easily it could be and has been said that all we are missing, the last part of the puzzle is self-accountability and initiative. Powerful as thought is it would be wise to fill it with the jewels of honest self-assessment and cultivation both from intuition as well as externals by which our intellect is strengthened. We are in the age of light and the only shadow are those we cast within our own mind bred by self-doubt and fear. Easily is the not the way of transformation but incredible is the journey and inevitable is the conclusion. The only magic is that of our own will and imagination. No ritual, no abracadabra or superficial objects can manifest the reality we truly want and deserve for abundance, peace and prosperity is our birthright. Evil is an illusion created by small minds that can't conceive anything better for themselves. The only truth is that of Love, Peace, Freedom and Justice which are tempered by the two greatest virtues by which all things are manifested and pushed forward: sincerity and consistency. Also, just so its stated, I am no medical doctor or supposed Guru of some sort. I am simply an informed and concerned man who wills that those who need will want and thus receive what they truly seek and that seeking align themselves with tranquility which is freedom. Wa Alaikum As Salaam.

These are a few Moor businesses that one should support:

- **Califamedia.com (literature and publishing)**

- **Rvbeypublications.com (literature)**

- **Dr. AlimElBey.com (herbs, crystals, literature and More)**

- **Moors and masonryr.org (etymology, history, jurisprudence)**

- **Publishedinfo.net (tools for war)**

- **Etymologyrules.com (Mind expansion)**

- **WillofAllah.com (music)**

- **Riseofthemoors.com**

- **Cordobaorganics.com (skin alchemy)**

- **Aseerthedukeoftiers.com (adept metaphysics)**

- **13Krystalign.com (cleanses and detoxes)**

- **Uprisingtea.com**

Final word

"A beggar nation cannot attain its highest level of spirituality". -Noble Drew Ali

Whether you realize it or not we are one and if we want strength we must be the backbone of each other. A billion cornerstones make a strong pyramid, but a single finger cannot lift much. These businesses are run by upstanding men and women, people with principles and morals who not only need our support but deserve it. They have given and continue to give much to our people and the world in general and the energies they represent, and manifest are some of the reasons we are still allowed to exist at all on this planet at all. They are the balance that shifts the scales in favor of Love, Truth, Peace, Freedom and Justice. Taking without giving is disgraceful and unbalanced and giving to those who have no true morals is even worse than not giving at all and must be rectified with knowledge, wisdom and overstanding. No one in this realm is without flaws but as Confucius once said, "better a diamond with a flaw than a pebble without", and these are true gems but, "only a jeweler can appreciate gems". Learn Moor, Think Moor, Do Moor, Be Moor. Wa Alaikum As Salaam.

The Golden Rule

Buddhism:
Hurt not others with that which pains yourself.

Christianity:
Do unto others as you would have them do unto you.

Hinduism:
Treat others as you would yourself be treated.

Islam:
Do unto all men as you would wish to have done unto you.

Judaism:
What you yourself hate, do to no man.

Native American:
Live in harmony, for we are all related.

Sacred Earth:
Do as you will, as long as you harm no one.

www.ingramcontent.com/pod-product-compliance
Lightning Source LLC
Chambersburg PA
CBHW080902130526
44591CB00050B/2450